How to Pass the Criminal Justice Oral Interview – 2ⁿᵈ Edition

Police and Fire Publishing
1800 N. Bristol St.
Suite C408
Santa Ana, Ca. 92707
Email: Steve@policeandfirepublishing.com
www.policeandfirepublishing.com
ISBN: 978-1-936986-13-2

Note to the reader: Concepts, principles, techniques, and opinions presented in this manual are provided as possible considerations. The application, use, or adoption of any concepts, principles, techniques, or opinions contained in this manual are at the risk of the individual or organization who makes that decision.

QR (Quick Response) codes

http://www.policeandfirepublishing.com

QR (Quick Response) codes incorporate advanced technology to deliver a reality-based application beyond the textbook. The subject matter "comes to life" through a video clip, complete with the sights and sounds unique to each chapter; each QR code offers a broader perspective of the material being taught and a better understanding of how it is applied in the field.

QR codes can be quickly accessed with a cell phone and are tailor-made for quick and easy linking to content on smart phones. Simply point the phone's camera at the QR code you wish to scan. There are a number of apps in the iPhone App Store that can read QR codes, including the free QR Reader. Most Android phones and Blackberries read the codes right out of the box, as can newer Nokia headsets. For older Androids and Blackberries, download free QR reader applications. Windows Mobile users can download Quick Marks.

Table of Contents

Oral Interview Questions

Introduction

This book is a supplement to *How to Get Hired in Criminal Justice*. You will be introduced to numerous oral interview questions that will familiarize you with the criminal justice mindset. You should not memorize the questions and answers. Instead, you will learn to think as if you are already in the criminal justice field. Some of the answers are written in the first person and some as if you were giving instructions to the actual oral panel. This is your opportunity to come up with your own answers while experiencing how the panel is evaluating you. The formula to succeed in the interview will be introduced and you will no longer be concerned with passing; you will be aiming for the high 90s. All criminal justice positions function with a similar mindset. Though you may not be interested in other professions listed in this book, I still encourage you to answer those particular interview questions.

In addition to this book, read as many interview books as you can get your hands on. Even more importantly, practice your answers out loud. You can Google criminal justice/law enforcement interviews and find numerous books on the subject. There is no "one" perfect book, but most will offer some type of insight. Understand that this book is not meant for you to memorize in order to answer like a robot; rather it is intended to get you thinking like a public safety professional. There are many ways to answer a question and it is imperative that you consider all options. The more you interact with others whom are interested in criminal justice/law enforcement, the more your mind will expand to handle any situation.

Chapter 1
Preparing for the Interview

Learning Objectives

1 • Understand necessary preparation required to succeed in a law enforcement interview

2 • Understand the small factors that can make or break you during the interview process

3 • Practicing and understanding difficult scenarios that might be asked, prior to the interview

http://www.youtube.com/watch?v=M-exbgCjioA

The "Phone Call"!

"This is Jane Doe from XYZ Police Department. I'm calling to schedule you for a job interview." Your pulse races; a job interview—it's finally here! It isn't until the night before the interview that your stomach drops and a feeling of slight dread sets in.

If this feeling is overwhelming, it is a strong indication you have not prepared well enough. Preparing for a public safety interview is a year-long process and it incorporates a vast amount of knowledge and common sense. Your learning institution cares about your success and understands the importance of preparation. Read, study, and discuss this book with peers, professors and actual criminal justice professionals and you will ace the oral interview.

Don't Forget Your Resumes!

Make good-quality copies of your resume on a nice grade of paper. Take more copies than you will possibly need—just in case, store the copies in a black dossier where they will stay clean and unwrinkled. Even if you attached a resume with your application the panel may not have it.

Organize a portfolio, tear sheets, professional reference lists, or any other papers you think your prospective employer would like to see. Make sure your purse or briefcase is stocked with everything else you'll need: a working pen (no pencils!), a notebook, breath mints, a comb, and some tissues.

Practice Makes Perfect

Like most things, people get better at interviewing with practice. Dedicate at least one night per month to participating in what is called a "mock interview." A mock interview is a question and answer session in which both the interviewer and the interviewee act as if it were a formal interview. You can set this up with a friend or conduct the interview yourself with a list of frequently-asked interview questions and a mirror.

Don't panic if, during the actual interview, you are not asked any of the questions you practiced. The point of practicing is to "warm up" to the process of answering questions on the fly.

Do Your Homework

Spend at least two months before the interview researching the company. Take notes. Memorize important facts and understand the culture of the organization.

A little preparation goes a long way. A couple months of researching the organization and practicing answers to interview questions can give you that extra bit of confidence you need to ace the interview.

An Interview Strategy: Telling Stories

If you read many books on job interviews, you'll notice that some feed you lists of interview questions that you should learn answers to. But an interview is not an interrogation; it's a conversation. Thus, the best way to prepare for an interview is to come armed with a multitude of small stories about both your business and personal life.

Conversation Wins the Job

Competency-based interviews, as opposed to traditional interviews, have become more common today. In a traditional interview, the interviewer will ask you questions focused on whether you have the skills and knowledge needed to do the job. A competency-based interview goes further by asking you additional questions about your character and personal attributes that can better determine whether you fit their corporate culture. These are called "behavioral competencies."

A competency-based interviewer will spend about half the interview on your job skills, and about half on your behavioral competencies. He or she will be looking for evidence of how you have acted in real situations in the past. So, having your stories ready and engaging in a conversation during the interview plays very well for this type of setting.

The Interviewer's Priorities

An employer wants to find out:

- ☐ Are you an asset or liability?

- ☐ Are you a team player? Will you fit into the corporate hierarchy or be like sand in the gears? Can you take and give (if appropriate) orders?

- ☐ Will you fit into the organizational culture?

They don't want primadonnas.

Story Strategy

A story is the best way to relay information in a positive way. You should have several stories that you can use as examples of your successes, and each story should have a message. Start by developing your stories around these areas:

☐ Examples of when you either made or saved money for your current or previous employer.

☐ A crisis in your life or job and how you responded or recovered from it.

☐ A time where you functioned as part of a team and what your contribution was.

☐ A time in your career or job where you had to overcome stress.

☐ A time in your job where you provided successful leadership or a sense of direction.

☐ A failure that occurred in your job and how you overcame it.

☐ Any seminal events that happened during your career to cause you to change direction and how that worked out for you.

Actions speak louder than words. Your actions in the past—relayed in story form—will tell a company much more than any generic response. Your stories will give the interviewer the tangible examples he or she seeks, and they will convey a strong sense of your individuality, making you stand out more.

How to Answer the Toughest Interview Questions

You know they're coming: Those seemingly unanswerable questions that pop up during job interviews. You can't clam up. And you don't want to stutter and stammer. So, what's a job seeker to do?

The "Future" Question

Otherwise known as the "big picture" question, the future question goes something like this: "where do you see yourself in five years?"

The best tactic: talk about your values.

Don't get too detailed about your specific career plan. Instead, discuss things that are important to you professionally and how you plan to achieve them. If growth is a goal, mention that. You can also talk about challenge, another value that employers prize in their employees.

The Seemingly Silly Question

If you were a tree, what kind of a tree would you be? What if you were a car? Or an animal? These types of questions can bring your interview to a screeching halt. First, don't panic. Pause, and take a deep breath. Then remind yourself that there's no "right" answer to these questions. The job isn't hinging on whether you choose to be a maple versus an oak.

Interviewers usually ask these questions to see how you react under pressure and how well you handle the unexpected. It's not so important what type of tree (or car, or animal) you choose, but rather that you explain your choice in a way that makes you look favorable.

So, be a maple—because you want to reach new heights in your career. Or be an oak—because you plan to put down roots at the company. Either way, you'll get it right.

How to Deal With Interview Stress

To many job seekers, the word "stress" is synonymous with "job interview." Job seekers stress over landing an interview. Then they stress over preparing for it. And then they stress over what to wear, what to say, if the interviewer will like them and more.

But the worst stress of all often occurs during the interview. This is the stress that can cause you to blow it. It can make you freeze, panic, chatter aimlessly, lose your train of thought or perspire profusely.

So, how can job seekers keep cool when it counts? Relax. A few simple techniques can help calm frayed nerves and sooth interview jitters.

Early Warning

Timing is everything: don't cause yourself undue stress before a big interview. Arrive early, but not too early—you'll sit and wait and worry. If you arrive too late, you may find yourself racing in the door, your heart already pounding from a last-minute dash.

A twenty-minute, pre-interview break will give you an opportunity to catch your breath and acclimate to your surroundings. It's enough time, but not too much time. We will cover this in greater detail later in the book.

Picture This

You can make your dream a reality. Use your imagination to stay calm during a job interview. Visualization is a relaxation technique in which you create a mental image of a stressful or challenging situation. Then you imagine yourself succeeding in the situation. By doing so, you're mentally preparing to handle the event in real life.

You can practice visualization in the days, hours, or even minutes before an interview. Simply close your eyes and breathe deeply. Picture yourself greeting the interviewer confidently and answering tough questions with ease. Practice succeeding in your imagination, and soon you'll be doing it in reality.

Relax

A relaxed job candidate is a confident job candidate. Show the interviewer that you're calm, composed, and in command during an interview. He's likely to assume that you'll be rock-solid on the job, too.

Use these tips to stay relaxed during an interview:

- Breathing deeply and slowly (and quietly, of course)
- Sit up straight and don't cross your legs or arms
- Speak slowly and pause for breath often
- Keep your hands and jaw relaxed; no clenching
- Smile—it really is contagious!

Pause, Don't Panic

In every interview, there comes a moment that doesn't go according to plan. There's an awkward silence. You stumble over your words. You flub a tough question. Don't panic. Now's the time to put your relaxation skills into overdrive. It's much easier to control fear and panic as it starts to build than to calm yourself down once they've begun to spiral out of control.

When you feel yourself starting to panic and lose focus, pause. Tell yourself silently that you can do it. Take a deep breath. Refocus. And then resume interviewing. A quick five-second pause can be all you need to regain your composure and get back in control. And the interviewer probably won't even notice.

How to Handle Illegal Interview Questions

Interviews are already stressful enough. Between promoting your skills, showing enthusiasm, and laughing at the interviewer's bad jokes, you have plenty to concentrate on.

But when you suspect you've been asked an illegal interview question—stress levels can shoot even higher.

Fortunately, if you know in advance what kind of illegal questions are most apt to sneak into an interview, you can diffuse the situation immediately and move on to more important tasks—like landing the job.

Three Ways to Answer Illegal Interview Questions

Most interviewers are not out to discriminate against job applicants. Many of the illegal questions that interviewers ask are unintentional—in fact, if you act surprised and tactfully point out that the question is illegal, the interviewer will likely realize his or her gaffe and immediately retract the question.

The challenge for you is to figure out what to say while you're sitting in that chair, faced with an illegal question. You have three basic options:

☐ Just answer the question. If you don't mind providing the information and you don't want to make waves, you can respond to the question and move on to the next one. Keep in mind, however, that you should only answer the question if you are truly comfortable with providing that information—it could come back to haunt you.

☐ Refuse to answer the question. Inform the interviewer that the question doesn't seem to be legal or relevant to the specific requirements of the job. Be forewarned, though, that such a direct response should really be saved for questions that are offensive, or deeply troubling.

☐ Don't answer the question, but answer the intent behind the question. This is usually the best option, since it allows you to provide a tactful answer without sacrificing your rights. To answer the intent behind the question, try to figure out what the interviewer REALLY wants to know. For example, if the interviewer asks if you are a U.S. citizen (which is an illegal question), a smart answer would be, "If you mean to ask if I am legally authorized to work for you, the answer is yes." In cases like these, it is best to rephrase the question into a legal one and then answer it. This displays flexibility and composure which are strong job skills.

Keep in mind if you are interviewing for a sworn position there are very few questions that are off-limits. You will be scrutinized beyond anything you have ever been through in your life and for good reason. As a public safety official you will be allowed into citizens' houses; they will hand you their choking baby or trust you with money and property. An intense background check ensures only the individuals with the highest of ethics will be hired. The panel is also evaluating whether or not you can handle its associated power.

Professional Advice: Answering Questions Related to a Sordid Past

Age Limit

Recent reports say that workers are planning to hold jobs well into their senior years. Many even plan to hold off retirement until their 70s or 80s in order to continue bringing in paychecks. Unfortunately, this has resulted in an increase in complaints from older workers of age discrimination in the workplace, according to the Equal Employment Opportunity.

The good news is that interviewers are not allowed to ask you your age during an interview. With some rare exceptions, the only age-related question they can ask you is if you're over the age of 18.

One thing to keep in mind: the EEOC's Age Discrimination in Employment Act of 1967 only protects workers who are 40 years old and older from age discrimination, and in workplaces with 20 or more employees. However, some local governments have laws that also encourage age discrimination rules for younger applicants and smaller workplaces.

However, can public safety set an age limit? The answer is yes, although it is not widespread. There has been extensive media coverage regarding 50 year olds completing the police academy in recent years.

Minor Matters That Make Your Interview

Preparing for an interview can be stressful and time-consuming. You can spend the final days before the interview researching a company, brainstorming answers to "trick" questions and preparing your portfolio. With so much to do, it's easy to forget the practical details that can distinguish a successful interview from a tragic one. This article focuses on the minor matters that job seekers often overlook before they sit down in the interview hot seat.

Supplemental Media: Expert Advice on Mitigating the Oral Interview

http://www.youtube.com/watch?v=PCFtNS5_UdY

http://www.youtube.com/watch?v=e9NjkypHn7E

Getting Your Interview Gear Ready

Lay out your clothing in advance. You don't want to be frantically searching for a missing sock or clean shirt on the day of the interview.

Make sure your suit is clean and neatly pressed and take care of other time-consuming chores (polishing your shoes, trimming your nails) the day before the interview if possible.

Also, gather all of the other important materials you'll need for the interview in one place, where you will be sure not to forget them. You might include copies of your resume, references, and directions.

Just Call Me "Dragon Breath"

Your parents were right: you don't do as well on an empty stomach. Make sure you eat before the interview. You don't need to have a huge meal. In fact, a heavy meal or one loaded with carbohydrates can make you feel sluggish and lethargic. But a light meal or snack will ensure that your stomach doesn't start grumbling loudly just as you're about to discuss your most brilliant accomplishment. We will cover this topic in greater detail later.

If your interview isn't until later in the day, steer clear of stinky bards, such as onions and garlic. Whatever you plan to eat before the interview should be followed by some mouthwash and a good brushing.

Have Interview, Will Travel

The day of the big interview is not the time to try out a new shortcut or investigate an unfamiliar area. Make sure you know how to get to your interview in advance. Make a practice run the day before if necessary.

Also, find out exactly where you'll need to go when you arrive at the department. If you're lucky, you'll walk through the front door and find the receptionist waiting. If you're not so lucky, you'll need to find your way to Lot 8, Building 9, Floor 10, Suite D, Room 125—so, be sure you know how to get there.

Eyes and Ears Are Everywhere

When it comes to interviewing, a little paranoia can be a good thing. Your interview starts in the parking lot, so be conscious of your surroundings. Any onlooker could be one of your interviewers. Act accordingly.

Be courteous and professional to everyone you meet, from the security guard to the receptionist. If you make small talk with strangers, be positive and pleasant. There isn't time to complain about the "funny smell in the lobby" or a long wait for an elevator.

Lastly, turn off your cell phone, or better yet—leave it in the car!

Six Common Job Interview Questions

One of the easiest ways to build confidence before a job interview is to prepare answers to questions you might be asked. Whether you're applying for a position as a police officer, firefighter, probation or parole officer, social worker, web programmer, accountant, or legal secretary, interviewers often utilize general questions to assess candidates, so you'll increase your chances if you prepare for them in advance.

Six common questions are listed below, along with insights from several recruitment professionals about how to answer. As part of your interview preparation, take the time to formulate answers to each question, focusing on specific tasks and accomplishments.

What are your strengths and weaknesses?

This is one of the most common interview questions, and interviewers often ask it indirectly, as in, "what did your most recent boss suggest as areas for improvement in your last performance review?"

Focus on skills that will benefit the prospective employer. Though you may have a knack for building houses, it might be of little value for the job at hand.
When it comes to weaknesses, or areas of growth, focus on how you have improved, and specifics about what you have done to improve yourself in those areas.

Why did you leave your last position?

Interviewers will always want to know your reasoning behind leaving a company, particularly if you are a job hopper. Tell the truth, without speaking negatively about past employment.

Can you describe a previous work situation in which you...?

This question comes in many forms, but what the interviewer is looking for is your behavior on the job. Your answer could focus on resolving a crisis, overcoming a negotiation deadlock, handling a problem coworker, or juggling multiple tasks on a project.

The theory behind this type of question is that past behavior is the best predictor of future behavior. Responding well is to real job examples and describing your behavior in specific situations will demonstrate important skills that the job requires.

What is your ideal work environment?

This question is not about whether you prefer a cubicle or an office, so think broadly to include ideas about supervision, management styles, and your workday routine.

This question reveals work habits, flexibility, and creativity.

How do you handle mistakes?

The best strategy for this question is to focus on one or two specific examples in the past and, if possible, highlight resolutions or actions that might have relevance to the job you're applying for.

What is your most notable accomplishment?

Practice three or four accomplishments and articulate what they meant in terms of increasing revenues, savings resources, or improving resources. Quantifying your achievements will place you above the rest.

Chapter 1 Discussion Questions

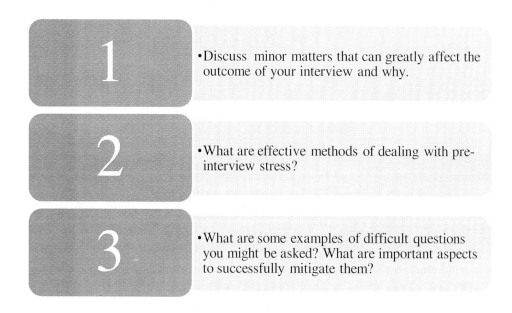

1
- Discuss minor matters that can greatly affect the outcome of your interview and why.

2
- What are effective methods of dealing with pre-interview stress?

3
- What are some examples of difficult questions you might be asked? What are important aspects to successfully mitigate them?

Chapter 2
The Day of the Interview

Learning Objectives

1
- Key components of your arrival, parking lot etiquette, and words to avoid during the interview

2
- All of the minor things you can do to ensure yourself the highest chance of success

3
- Being yourself and how taking advice from others can work against you

The Day of the Interview

If you have a morning appointment time, wake up early and eat a light breakfast. If your appointment is in the afternoon, make sure you are well-rested. I also recommend having a great workout about three hours before your interview. It will release tension and provide a positive-feel-good energy for the day.

Listen to yourself one more time with an audiotape of your opening and closing statements. Watch our DVD one more time to ensure you are totally familiar with the content. Be confident as this is the day you launch your career. You can't wait to speak with the panel to show them how well you have prepared!

The Arrival

http://www.youtube.com/watch?v=hKzOMnOIIfo

Interviews should not be intimidating if you are properly prepared. The first thing you must do is get there on time; remember, it's better to be one hour early than one minute late. If you are in an unfamiliar area you should leave early. It would be wise to drive the route the night before the interview, but be sure to account for traffic during the day. You should arrive in the parking lot approximately forty-five minutes to an hour early, as that will give you built-in extra time in case you hit a major accident or construction on the way. If you are early you can sit in the reception area and soak up the atmosphere and culture of the department. How do they act, dress, talk, etc.? This will give you an edge and

insight on how the department works. You should arrive at the office about fifteen to twenty minutes early; which indicates that you are a punctual individual. Do not check in too early as it could be construed as "weird."
Don't be late!

Tardiness promotes a self-centered attitude.

Being on hundreds of interview panels, I can tell you, nothing bothers a panel more than an applicant being a few minutes late. There are numerous applicants with scheduled interview slots. You will delay the panel, and the other candidates, and it will reflect so poorly on you that you may not be able to overcome it. You may think this is a little bit too strict, but imagine being on an interview panel for several days; you're sick and tired of listening to the same speech and the same answers over and over again. Believe me when I tell you, it doesn't take much to become irritated at this point. Tardiness is the epitome of being self-centered and irresponsible and will push all of the other appointments back. If the unlikely situation occurs and you will be late, you must call at least 30 minutes in advance and notify the personnel representative of what occurred.

This will slightly mitigate the fact that you are late, but why take the chance? Be on time! Take my advice and show up substantially early and do not allow being late to be a factor in success or failure.

The Parking Lot

Think about your oral while sitting in the car, recite your introduction and be natural. When the appointment is approximately 30 minutes away make your way into the building. Make believe that you have a camera focused on your every move; a panel member could be looking into the parking lot from the office window at that very moment. They could be parking their vehicle next to you. It will be obvious why you are there, and you will be watched. Take your time walking into the building, relax, there is no rush because you left early. Use the restroom, wash your hands, look at your suit and tie for drips of breakfast or coffee stains. Check in with the receptionist approximately 20 minutes before your appointment and calmly watch the rushed applicants.

http://www.youtube.com/watch?v=NutNd9Ow_EY

Preparing for the Oral Interview

Make sure your application is perfect. Have other trusted sources proofread your written work. You may not realize it, but you have actually set the tone of the interview with the professionalism of the application. A poorly written or sloppy application will elicit additional scrutiny by the panel.

Well-intentioned Assistance

Some people love to give advice; keep in mind that many of them are full of bad advice. You should be very selective in whom you choose as your mentor and filter advice several different ways. They may have begun their career before IQ mattered, or be a disgruntled employee. Some employees may adopt a culture that does not necessarily reflect the mission of the organization. They were probably hired before a polygraph and psychological examination were part of the hiring process. Utilize common sense and you will do well.

I constantly hear the advice applicants receive from well-meaning employees; almost all of it is wrong! I've also received information that many colleges are teaching improper criminal justice interview techniques in their classes. I believe in education, but you have to remember public safety is different from the civilian world and some professors do not understand the culture involved. So pay attention to this book!

Read this book closely and utilize the tips from public safety officials who are actually on interview panels. True experts from the field are giving you factual, real-world advice, helping you achieve your goal!

http://www.youtube.com/watch?v=Jo1opZa1dy4

According to a cross section of hiring officials who have cumulatively conducted thousands of oral interview panels, there are a few things you can do to improve your odds for a successful interview:

- Be confident from the moment you walk in the building; a lack of confidence is a recipe for disaster.

- Maintain a professional and friendly demeanor. This gives more authority than a badge ever will.

- Be friendly. Being likeable and positive is the key to almost everything successful in life.

- Display loyalty. Do not bad mouth prior jobs or co-workers

- Be honest. Admit mistakes and explain how you have improved since then.

- Say what you believe. Do not say what you think the panel wants to hear because you may be wrong.

- Send thank you notes. They suggest:
    - You are a people person
    - The employer remembers you
    - It will impress them
    - Reiterates your interest
    - Correct any wrong impressions left
    - Class

There are also a few things you should absolutely never do during an interview. Do not:

- [ ] Chew gum

- [ ] Eat a garlic laden meal the day of the interview

- [ ] Smoke the day of the interview

- [ ] Wear too much cologne

- [ ] Crack your knuckles

- [ ] Leave your cell phone on

- [ ] Turn your back to an interviewer, even slightly

- [ ] Ask questions at the end of the interview, unless they pertain to the selection process

- [ ] Interrupt panel members

- [ ] Use fillers repeatedly, such as: "um," "like," "okay," "ya know," and "yeah"

One applicant actually answered his cell phone during the interview. Hopefully it was from a prospective employer as he will not be working here!

Chapter 2 Discussion Questions

1
- Discuss things you can do as well as avoid doing to increase your chances of a successful interview.

2
- How can taking advice from others affect the outcome of the interview process?

3
- How can your behavior in the parking lot and prior to entering the actual interview affect the outcome?

Chapter 3
Preparation for the Interview

Learning Objectives

1. • Key components to a successful entry and conveying confidence

2. • Key aspects of a successful introduction and opening statement

3. • Exactly what skills the panel is looking for and how to demonstrate them effectively

Preparation

Preparation for the interview demonstrates to the panel what type of employee you will be. You can control most of the basics of the interview. One way to prove your worth and preparation is to carry a dossier with you. When an opportunity to discuss a project you have completed or a major accomplishment you have achieved arises, seize the moment and offer a copy of the project. Chances are they will not take you up on the offer, but they will be impressed.

The Oral Interview Panel

The panel is usually comprised of sworn personnel who range from thirty-five to fifty years old. They are generally high achievers that have developed good reputations with the personnel section. On occasion they will play roles, one will be the nice guy and one will play the bad guy (good cop, bad cop). Many times they do not even know they are doing this and it almost always strikes a balance during the interview. The way you deal with a difficult panel member is to do absolutely nothing. Do not change the way you have been training. Give him/her the same amount of attention and respect you are giving the others. Remember that it isn't only your answers that are being tested, it's also your personality and how you handle adversity.

You also want to be yourself during the interview. Do not conform to what you think they may way because if you were conforming and not being yourself, would you really want to be hired like that? And you could be wrong!

Entry

Upon being summoned by the secretary for your appointment, walk in confidently, be careful not to slam the door, but don't shut the door so slowly that it appears you lack confidence in yourself. This is going to sound comical, but practice this just as you would anything else.

Greeting

http://www.youtube.com/watch?v=x__jDufdU0s

Greet the person nearest you with a solid firm handshake reaching the back of the palm. You go to the next closest person giving a firm handshake. Ensure that you look directly into the eyes of each person, which exudes confidence. Give a personal greeting such as, "nice to meet you," or "good morning," "pleasure to meet you," or any greeting you prefer. You may have sweaty palms due to nervousness; don't worry too much about this because it is very common and panel members are used to it. However, if you are aware of this problem and it's like shaking hands with a bucket of water, carry a handkerchief and wipe your hands as you are walking toward the interview room and put it into your pocket prior to entering. Practice doing this so you don't fumble when the real interview comes. You make break out in hives, or turn bright red; don't worry about these types of things. We know how nervous you are and how important the interview is to you. This is very common and we don't think anything of it.

As you sit down you may be so nervous that your mouth goes dry or you feel compelled to cough or clear your throat due to being uncomfortable. If this is a common occurrence for you, bring a small bottle of water to sip during the interview. If you do cough, please do us all a favor and use your left hand to conduct your sanitary business. When you use your right hand to cover your mouth or wipe the white stuff from around your lips, it is difficult to think of anything else because soon we will be shaking hands. To understand exactly what I'm talking about, rent the movie *Philadelphia*. There is a powerful scene in which an AIDS victim, played by Tom Hanks, is at an attorney's office, played by Denzel Washington. The camera hones in on each object Hank's character touches, and expertly shows Washington's nervousness and uneasiness. This is exactly what a panel member goes through when you use your right hand.

It is proper to wait for the formality of being asked to have a seat before you sit down; and when you sit down, keep your feet flat on the floor and act natural without slouching!

Introduction and Opening Statement

Perfect position at the beginning of the interview

The first thing you will be asked by the oral panel is to talk about yourself. The panel will ask the question in many forms, such as: "John, tell us a little bit about yourself," "John, tell us about yourself and how you have prepared for the position," "John, what makes you qualified for this position?" Consider any of these questions an opportunity to give what is called a "hero statement." Do not minimize the importance of the opening statement. It sets the tone of the interview and establishes how serious you are about the job.

Explain how you have prepared for this position and don't be a robot. Let your personality shine through. It should sound something like this: "Hello, my name is Jonathan Smith. Two years ago I graduated from XYZ University with a Bachelor's Degree in mathematics. I became interested in the fire safety service when I was eight years old and saw the movie *Back Draft*. From that point on I studied everything I could get my hands on regarding firefighting. Immediately after high school I enrolled at XYZ Community College Fire Academy and finished #3 out of 60 candidates and was awarded, 'most likely to become a firefighter' by the academy staff.

I knew achieving my goal would be difficult as I had recently married and started a family, but I have financially prepared to follow my dream. I am extremely proud of this accomplishment as I continued fulfilling my reserve firefighting duties at the ABC Fire Department where I've been taking in as much knowledge and experience as I possibly can. [Talk about experience here] Working with firefighters and management personnel, I understand the culture of this department and I believe I fit in very well. I give you my word that I will give you 100% if given this opportunity." REMEMBER, YOU MUST SELL YOURSELF!

*Be sure to highlight your education
during the interview*

http://www.youtube.com/watch?v=I331FCOnO7o

http://www.youtube.com/watch?v=GSaNsj7E5_Q

Research

Most likely the next question you will be asked is "What can you tell me about our agency?" Or "What do you know about this agency?" Or "Why did you decide to apply here?" You should know the city and state, the demographics, political environment, and the department's philosophy.

Research can be in many mediums

You have many resources at your fingertips (i.e. internet), use them! If you have an opportunity to visit the department and/or go on a ride along, you can incorporate that into the interview. Name dropping is extremely effective if it is legitimate and you actually know the person. Warning: nothing makes a person look sillier than name dropping with no other reason than to bring the name up and ingratiate themselves to the panel. If you use someone's name, make sure to have a solid reason behind bringing it up, and you should have asked permission from the individual to use his or her name. There is a caveat though about name dropping. If the panel member does not like or respect the person you brought up, it will definitely be a disadvantage.

http://www.youtube.com/watch?v=2uHVoNOHSCk

Below is an actual document of instructions given to the panel members.

The following skills are related in the interview:
Communication Skills (included non-verbal):

☐ Articulation
☐ Demeanor/appearance
☐ Eye contact
☐ Listening skills (did they understand the question, did they ask us to repeat questions frequently, etc.)

An exceptional candidate in this area would have good eye contact with each member of the panel; would be able to articulate their thoughts effectively; their speech should not be monotone and should be understandable; would use appropriate English usage; would listen carefully and understand the questions presented and answer them accordingly; would have a professional demeanor and would try to stay calm (nerves are, of course, expected, but they should be able to control them as much as they can).

Decision Making Skills:

☐ Thought process
☐ Common sense
☐ Generating solutions or recommendations
☐ Evaluating consequences of actions

An exceptional candidate in this area would have a good thought process; they would have good common sense and would be able to quickly think of a solution or solutions; would be able to make decisions and stick with them (versus changing their mind several times); overall they should attempt to solve the problem—giving an "I don't know" answer is not acceptable.

Interpersonal Skills:
- ☐ Interaction with a diverse community & co-workers
- ☐ Direction from training officer and supervisors
- ☐ Ethics/morals
- ☐ Tactfulness & self-restraint

An exceptional candidate in this area would be able to effectively and tactfully interact with a diverse community; they would be able to work well with their peers and employees; they must be able to take direction well from their training officer and supervisor; must be able to follow a chain of command and/or adapt well to a paramilitary organization; must have high morals and ethics (Officers' ethics must be held at a higher standard than those of a civilian); must not overuse his authority or power.

These are some general areas taken into consideration:
- ☐ Basic background of the candidate
- ☐ Interest/motivation
- ☐ Community involvement/awareness
- ☐ Tactics/problem solving
- ☐ Ethics

Ensure the level of force is commensurate with the threat. Develop a thorough understanding of why you would or would not use force and to what extent. Remember, you are mandated by law and department policy to use the minimum amount of force necessary, but there will be times when force is necessary. Note: we remind candidates that experience or knowledge in certain areas is not expected. We do not expect them to know policies and procedures or specific tactical approaches. We tell them to base their answers on the knowledge they have acquired. Bottom line is: are they trainable? There are certain things we can teach them and certain things we cannot.

Here are some examples of general scenarios that candidates may be asked:

☐ Must know about the city and department they could potentially serve. Some agencies look for knowledge of mission statement and/or policing philosophy

☐ Why are they interested in a career in law enforcement? What have they done to show how serious they are about the career?

☐ Problems among neighbors. How can the officer assist them so they can reach an amicable solution?

☐ Problems among the entire neighborhood. How does the officer assist the entire neighborhood? How can the officer help them help themselves?

☐ Reoccurring problems where factors of the environment need to be changed in order to improve the image of a neighborhood or area. What changes can the officer suggest? What resources will he/she use?

☐ Off duty situations. What will the officer do if confronted with a problem when he/she is off duty?

☐ Encountering problems when the officer is outnumbered. What will he/she do? (Look for officer safety, but also public safety. Sometimes, depending on the nature of the problem, the officer may have to swallow his/her pride).

☐ Situations where an officer observes something that is unethical. What will the officer do? If it involves a friend, relative, co-worker, or even a supervisor, will they say something? (Basically, will they do the right thing even when no one is watching?)

Chapter 3 Discussion Questions

1

- Identify the major communication skills that will be looked for and how to demonstrate them effectively.

2

- Identify the interpersonal skills that will be looked for and how to demonstrate them effectively.

3

- Identify the decision making skills that will be looked for and how to demonstrate them effectively.

Chapter 4
What is the Panel Looking For

Learning Objectives

1
- 4 major conveyances that will need to be communicated to the panel to set you apart from the other applicants

2
- Successfully conveying reasons for becoming a police officer

3
- Explaining your life experiences and how they have prepared you for the job

The Panel

The panel may, or may not be in uniform.

There are four major conveyances that should be communicated to the oral interview panel.

1. Why are you here?
2. What can you do for us?
3. What type of person are you?
4. What distinguishes you from the other applicants?

Utilize the margins of each page to write notes and suggestions that remind you of additional research you must do.

Interview with a hiring panel

http://www.youtube.com/watch?v=1O2OzYvtZPs

44

The opening question can be asked in a number of different ways. Below are several of the most common opening questions, however do not let it divert you from the real focus, which is to tell them about yourself. Let some of the pressure figuratively transfer to the panel; they also need to find employees that fit with their organizational culture. The costs of hiring a bad employee in the private sector can exceed $50,000, which is nothing to sneeze at; however, a bad hire in the public safety sector can cost millions!

Who inspired you to become a police officer?

This question allows you to shine if you handle it well. "I was a young boy when I watched a police officer arrest a drug dealer in my neighborhood. The area immediately improved and I personally saw the power of one individual change a neighborhood. I want to change bad neighborhoods into good ones. I graduated high school with the knowledge that I would someday be a police officer. I entered the United States Army where I completed my Associate's Degree in Criminal Justice. I was also promoted to the rank of Sergeant before I was honorably discharged. I continued my education obtaining my Bachelor's Degree in Communication at XYZ College. While attending college, I worked full time at McDonald's where I was promoted to lead cashier in less than a year. It was during this time that I honed my people skills; I was selected by the manager to mitigate any issues that arose with unhappy customers. I have trained in martial arts and I am both mentally and physically ready for the academy."

Were there any specific times in your life when you recall thinking, "I want to become a police officer"?

"Yes, I was fifteen years old when I saw a drive-by shooting happen on my way home from school. An officer observed the shooting and quickly apprehended the shooters. It was impressive and began my interest in law enforcement. The area immediately improved and I personally saw the power of one individual change a neighborhood. I want to change bad neighborhoods into good ones. I graduated high school with the knowledge that I would someday be a police officer. I entered the United States Army where I completed my Associate's Degree in Criminal Justice. I was also promoted to the rank of Sergeant before I was honorably discharged. I continued my education obtaining my Bachelor's Degree in Communication at XYZ College. While attending college, I worked full time at McDonald's where I was promoted to lead cashier in less than a year. It was during this time that I honed my people skills; I was selected by the manager to mitigate any issues that arose with unhappy customers. I have trained in martial arts and I am both mentally and physically ready for the academy."

The above paragraph was not a mistake. Hopefully you noticed the same paragraph to a different question. This is how you will train and excel in the interview. Anytime you can tie in your training experience and education into an answer you should.

Why do you want to become a Police Officer?

This can vary from person to person; you have a story, tell it from your heart. The standard answer is "I want to help people." That answer is fine and most of the time genuine. However, keeping the answer that simple is too vague and a waste of a golden opportunity. You will need to dig down and find the real reason and articulate it to the panel. What brought you to this point? Why are you willing to risk your life for people you don't even know and some who dislike the police?

Write down what you have accomplished and then use it in an opening statement.

What types of issues will you face in Law Enforcement and are you prepared for the associated pressures of being a Police Officer?

If you know any police officers this is the perfect opportunity to discuss the influence they have had on you. It is important that you acknowledge the pressures and how they will affect you. Shift work, danger, smaller circle of friends, and being told a "ticket story" everywhere you go (This should get a chuckle). Explain how you have considered each and every one of these issues and are more than willing to accept any negative consequences to fulfill what you are supposed to do in life.

Give us an example of a stressful situation you were in and how you dealt with it.

 This question is a gold mine if handled properly. Explain a situation or incident that occurred at work, home, or on the athletic field where you stepped up and minimized or solved the crisis. It could be a paperwork issue in the office, or elevated tensions among coworkers. It may be more dramatic as in a crime in progress in which you called the police and arranged the capture of suspects. Whatever the case, make it interesting and a positive reflection on your actions.

Chapter 4 Discussion Questions

1

- What are the 4 major things you will need to convey to the panel?

2

- What information is the panel looking for when they ask you why you want to be a police officer?

3

- What key factor is the panel looking for when they ask you about a stressful situation?

Chapter 5
Situational and Ethical Questions

Learning Objectives

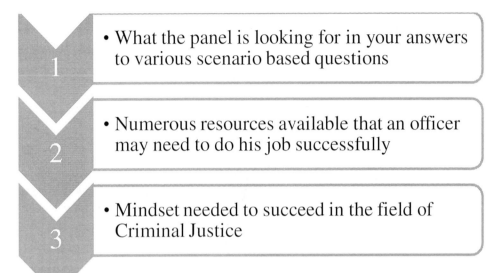

1 • What the panel is looking for in your answers to various scenario based questions

2 • Numerous resources available that an officer may need to do his job successfully

3 • Mindset needed to succeed in the field of Criminal Justice

Officer Oral Situational Questions

You will review actual oral interview questions from many years ago. In no way, shape, or form am I trying to give you questions that are currently being used. What I am trying to do is assist you in developing a certain mindset that you must have to succeed in public safety. These multiple scenarios will help you open your mind and determine your level and where you should focus your studies.

During the situational questions you will have the opportunity to display your analytical skills and discuss the research you've conducted on each subject. You'll need to "think out loud," showing your thought process. Don't make the panel guess what you're thinking!

Most agencies use situational questions which are asked to test your logic and reasoning. There are no right answers, but there are definitely wrong answers. Think logically and out loud.

Most candidates for law enforcement do not understand the importance of utilizing good judgment and fairness. It is vital that you understand that you will be initiating court proceedings which may lock people up for the rest of their lives. You must ALWAYS do the right thing.

Jail and the Responsibility of Authority

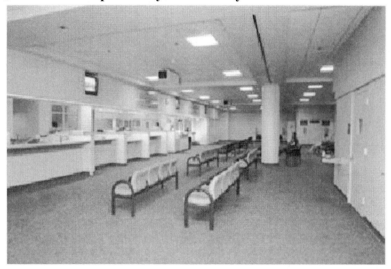

This city jail is like many other institutions in which your arrestees will be housed. The panel is evaluating many attributes, but one of the most important is fairness. If you are selected as a police officer you will have the ability to take away a person's liberty. Can you be trusted to use this power in a fair and unbiased manner?

Typical Jail Cell

Prison

Prison is an institution that houses inmates for terms of over one year.

An Interview is an Interview

It doesn't really matter which public safety profession you are entering; following this book will teach you how to ace any interview, any time! Police, fire, probation, corrections, etc. Do not skip over a question if you believe it does not pertain to you. Broadening your horizons is important in any endeavor. Attempts to answer areas of expertise you are unfamiliar with can only make you a better interviewer. Remember to stop talking when you've made your point clear and abide by the old saying, "you sold it, don't buy it back."

Read through this book several times and practice it with anyone that will assist you. The feedback given to you by people that have no knowledge of criminal justice is invaluable and will force you to explain your answers and engage in a conversation. If you can make the interview seem like a natural conversation you will do exceptionally well on your score. Good Luck!

Practical application scenarios and resources:

☐ Intellect, common sense, and compassion are the most important, however a criminal justice professional should be familiar with all available resources. The answers are framed in first and third person perspectives to help you more thoroughly understand the interview process.

Tools of the Trade

There are numerous resources a police officer can utilize when performing their job. The following are just a few of them.

PR-24, Handcuffs

Police unit and its associated safety features

Helicopter

Helicopters have been used in law enforcement for several decades and have saved lives, of both officers and suspects. Infrared helicopters can scan the terrain for body heat, keeping officers on the ground from walking into an ambush.

Record Checks

If you know the person's name and/or address a computer check will often pay dividends; information is your friend and can only enhance and further justify any decision you make.

Canine

There are several different breeds used by police departments and military personnel. Canines provide an invaluable safety tool as they are trained to locate, bite, and sniff out explosives in a systematic search. Canines significantly increase officer safety.

Harbor Patrol

Can be utilized in bodies of water, i.e searching for disposed bodies, etc.
Harbor Patrol protects citizens in beach areas.

Pepper spray- is used on violent and aggressive subjects.

Taser- used when pepper spray may be ineffective.

Probation and parole officers as well as police officers work closely with these individuals often utilizing their respective resources forming a symbiotic existence.

Other officers- they come from all walks of life and have a litany of skills. Get to know your teammates and utilize their expertise to its fullest.

Supervisors- usually a wealth of experience and they are willing to share it with you.

Telephone/texting- if you need to communicate with a group of young people, texting is the fastest way to disseminate information. Older people may not be familiar with new technology and you must find other methods of communication.

Tow trucks remove vehicles and hazards from the roadway.

S.W.A.T. Team (Special Weapons and Tactics Team)

Utilize S.W.A.T. when necessary, however, articulate to the panel that there will be a time delay and continue to deal with the situation that is unfolding in front of you.

You witness a minor traffic violation and attempt to initiate a vehicle stop. The vehicle continues on for approximately half a block and pulls into a residential garage. He closes the garage door behind him and refuses to come out. Prior to this you were able to get a good look at the driver and the license plate comes back registered to your current location. What would you do?

Call in the license plate and location; it makes a big difference if the driver knew he was being stopped by a police officer or not. Call for back up and then knock on the door and/or ring the doorbell. Call into the house with the name of the registered owner of the vehicle. (They will only ask a follow up question if you fail to fully answer the question)

Follow-up: What if, when you knock on the door, no body answers? What if you see, out of the corner of your eye, the man peeking out from behind the curtain?

There is a legal argument for kicking in the door and arresting the man; but really, would that be the best way to handle this situation? Call a supervisor, obtain his phone number and call inside and attempt to talk him out of the house. If you are unsuccessful, document the incident, obtain a DMV photo and present the case to the district attorney for filing or contact at a later time. This answer demonstrates that you can differentiate between exigency and a minor grade crime.

If the driver fails to answer the door and it appears he knows we are there, I would consider entry into the residence. I most likely would not force entry due to the minimal nature of the crime; a possible evading is all I have. I would, however, file a crime report and if I could identify him from a license photograph. Then seek a warrant for his arrest and possibly send him a citation in the mail.

You respond to a service call regarding a neighbor dispute. Upon arrival you learn two neighbors are having a disagreement over their property line where one neighbor wants to plant a tree. There have been no criminal violations. What, if anything, would you do?

Just wait to see if the applicant will attempt to mediate or resolve the situation instead of just leaving when he learns there are no criminal violations. Could he refer them to either a city or county surveyor? Can he research case law and determine if a precedent has been established for this situation.

Follow-up: What if they start to get angry with each other and begin poking each other in the chest?

This would be considered assault and they may be subject to arrest, but keeping it civil will be in the best interest of all concerned.

Would this be overreaction in a civil case? Maybe; maybe not. Does the officer believe him to be armed? Has he shown signs of hostility? Does he have a history of violence? Don't be so quick to judge.

Mentally Challenged Individuals

It is common for mentally challenged individuals to be enamored by the badge. Be careful how you respond to what may be perceived as aggressiveness, but is actually fondness and admiration. Doctors and mental health professionals may have personal knowledge of the mentally ill person you are dealing with, and can calm a situation.

You receive a call from a mentally challenged female who lives in a group home. She tells you her group home advisor forced her to have sexual relations with him two weeks ago. What will you do?

Well, first I have to take this allegation seriously because it is not beyond the realm of possibility that it actually occurred. I would take her to an area where she feels safe and obtain specific details. I would also take her for a medical examination and collect any clothes she was wearing that day, as well as bedding and any other objects that may have been involved. I would contact her social worker and gather further information. I would then conduct an interview with the group advisor, whether or not he was a suspect. I would be ever mindful that I am the victim's voice. If there was a crime I could prove I would arrest the responsible person. I would work with the social worker to find acceptable accommodations for the victim.

Teenage Runaway

You get a call to take a report of a missing person. You proceed to the address given to you and speak to a woman who says that her 15-year-old daughter has run away. This girl has run away several times previously, but always comes home on her own after a few days. Her mother is a chronic alcoholic and it's a bad home life for the girl. After you get the information needed for a report from the mother, you go back to the station. There you happen to mention this case to a fellow officer who used to be in charge of the police explorer program. The runaway used to be a police explorer, so you think that the officer may have some idea of where she might go when she leaves home. The officer tells you that he had developed a close "father-daughter" relationship with the girl when she was in the Explorers. He says he has allowed her to stay at his home when things get bad at her home. In fact, he tells you, the girl is at his home now. How would you wrap things up now that you know where the girl is?

The officer's behavior is simply unacceptable. He may think he is helping, but he is actually exacerbating the situation. Having her stay there with or without the mother's permission is a horrendous mistake and is possibly a crime; at the very least the perception of impropriety and ridicule from the public will undoubtedly occur. Call your supervisor immediately and send another police unit to his house to locate the missing person. If his assistance truly was for altruistic reasons it will come out in the internal affairs investigation. Refer the mother and daughter for family counseling and if determined that the home is unfit, I would lodge the teenager in a county facility for youth.

Follow-up: You are a junior officer and he is a senior officer. He says he has told his supervisor and called her mother. What if the officer truly convinced you that he was trying to be a Good Samaritan and he is now concerned that you're going to get him in trouble?

Do not change your answer. It is what it is. He made a mistake and the department will now determine the truth of the investigation.

Important tip: When a follow-up question leads you to believe you may have give the incorrect answer, whatever you do, do not change your answer! The best answer you can give is to say, "I considered that, but decided not to utilize that specific course of action because of X, Y, and Z."

You are dispatched to a possible stalled vehicle in the middle of a busy intersection. When you arrive you discover there is a suicidal female who has locked herself in her car. She is currently holding a gun to her head. She is apparently despondent over a recent divorce. She refuses to exit the car. What actions would you take?

Call for help and establish communications, possible resources such as a hostage negotiator. I would try to obtain her name either by asking or by her license plate. At the same time I would reassure her everything would be okay and gently persuade her to put the gun down and allow me to provide her with help.

Options

This is the safest way to take a suspect into custody. Control the situation and let him come to you. When unsure of a situation slow it down and take it step-by-step.

You pull over a vehicle for expired registration. As you approach the driver, he locks himself inside the car and ignores your request to open the doors. A small crowd has gathered and begins to encourage the man to drive away. The crowd is now yelling at you to leave the man alone because he hasn't bothered anyone. What action would you take?

Call for back up and a supervisor. Advise the crowd to move on and attempt to open all of the doors as he may have left one of them open. Contact a tow truck for a Slim Jim to open the car door. I don't know if this is tactically correct, but one option is to drive a police car in front of the vehicle and use the push bars to lock it in. Continue to reason with the driver for a peaceful conclusion. See if there are any missing person reports or mentally ill subjects that are wanted. The vehicle registration will give further indicators into a possible record and/or drug use.

Follow-up: Someone in the crowd has thrown a bottle at the police car and the crowd is now making hostile remarks towards you. What action would you take?

Call for emergency backup and radio in a description of the person that threw the bottle and his current location and direction of travel. Order the crowd to disperse or face arrest; at the same time do not forget about the primary issue; the driver is still in the car. When your backup arrives advise him or her of the situation and determine if you need additional units to handle multiple situations.

You are at a sandwich restaurant at a walk-up window. The cashier says, "Your food is on the house." Departmental policy states you cannot accept gratuities. What will you do?

Explain to the cashier that you appreciate the offer, but cannot accept it as your chief does not allow you to accept gratuities and attempt to pay for the meal.

Follow-up: The cashier emphatically states he is the owner and will be offended if you do not accept his gift.

You need to emphasize that you understand different cultures and not accepting the food could be considered a major insult by the owner. You, of course, do not want to alienate a business owner, so you explain the perception of accepting free food and how it could damage credibility with the public. Ultimately, if necessary, accept the sandwich and drop the full amount of the meal into a tip jar or a donation box for a charity on the counter. Let the area sergeant know what occurred and do your best to avoid uncomfortable situations in the future.

A woman comes up to you at the courthouse steps and explains to you that she saw a man with a gun go into one of the buildings. How would you handle the situation?

This is obviously a very serious situation and must be addressed immediately. Ask the lady for identification so you will have proof of a witness; get a better description of the gunman. Have her wait in a safe area. Notify dispatch of the situation and where the witness can be located. Have dispatch call inside the building and advise them of the incident. Call for backup and while waiting for backup attempt to get a view of the entrance of the building and contact an officer or security guard inside. Speak with the officers inside and work with them to ensure the safety of the occupants inside. They may have lockdown procedures and/or a specific manner of evacuation. At this time you will coordinate a search for the gunman, unless the gunman was deemed to be an officer displaying his/her weapon unintentionally. If this appears to be the case, have him/her walk outside in view of the witness for confirmation.

Burglary alarm, ransacked store; officer places a couple of lawn chairs in the trunk of his police vehicle. What will you do?

This is totally unacceptable and you need to stop the behavior immediately. Ask the officer what he is doing and listen intently to any answer he gives. Let's say, for example, that he says "These are the last two chairs like this and my wife was looking at them earlier today. I left the money on the counter." You proceed directly to the counter and there is more than enough to cover the cost of the chairs. Now, it is possible that there is not an ethical situation here, but definitely a perception problem if anyone were to see the officer removing the property.

Call a supervisor and advise him or her of the situation in the presence of the other officer. More than likely the sergeant will counsel and document the incident and explain the issue to the other officer.

You're on patrol and pull over a drunk driver who pulls into a driveway and stops in the parking lot. You call in the stop and advise dispatch that the location is in the church parking lot. The male subject gets out of the vehicle and you realize he is a priest who is obviously under the influence of alcohol. The father pleads for your forgiveness and says he has had a horrendous day. He says if you forgive him he will go into the church rectory (where he lives) and go to sleep.

Yes, he is home, but he had to drive to get there. The priest may have a problem with alcohol, and that is not for you to determine. You need to determine if he violated the law. You must make the arrest and, yes, it will be difficult, and you will be scrutinized, but imagine if you let him slide and the next time he gets behind the wheel drunk he kills people. What you do or don't do has ramifications, and if you do it right, you will never know the tragedies prevented. Of course, you will treat the priest with the utmost respect and notify a supervisor of the situation. When he gets to jail he will be separated from the other inmates, once again, out of courtesy.

You're driving with your training officer and a pursuit is announced over the radio. Your Field Training Officer (FTO) suggests you to parallel the pursuit. While doing so, speeds get a little out of hand, and you hit a curb causing damage to the tire and the rim of your unit. The FTO advises you to drive to the city yard and calls for a supervisor. When reporting the incident to the supervisor the FTO gives a different location for the incident. He later tells you he did that to cover your tracks for paralleling the pursuit which you shouldn't have advised and by simply changing the location it will not become an issue.

He tells you there is no damage to any other property, only the tire and rim on your unit, and you do not have to thank him because he knows you would do the same for him. How would you handle this situation?

This is unacceptable. Deceit will invalidate our credibility and undermine our authority. I will speak with the FTO and explain the discomfort and my wish to report the incident to a supervisor. If he or she attempts to intimidate me, or refuses to report the incident I would seek out my supervisor immediately and report the incident and the conversation afterward. I know this will make life difficult for me, but I also know many officers will respect me for doing the right thing.

Ethical Question During Interview

http://www.youtube.com/watch?v=DY_4TEp_Rtw

You are on probation and have been told by your supervisor that you're at the point of your career where you should not need to call him or other officers to handle routine situations like traffic stops. You're out the next night and you and your supervisor are the only officers on your team. You make a car stop for a traffic violation and after ten to fifteen minutes you cannot find the section to complete the ticket. The violator is taunting you that you're a rookie and do not know what you are doing. What are some possible solutions?

When I pull someone over I will definitely know why, but it is possible not to know the specific section. I would call another officer on my cell phone, the station supervisor, and even dispatch. I could write the violation and amend it later that night with a mailed notice, or I could simply let him or her go with a warning. Most likely I would swallow my pride and call my supervisor on the radio and ask him or her.

You make a traffic stop for a vehicle running a red light. Upon contact with the driver, you see that it is an elderly lady extremely scared and nervous, and possibly disoriented. You request her driver's license and she does not acknowledge your presence. Her windows are rolled up and she rigidly looks straight ahead and is visibly shaken. What would you do, and what are your concerns?

At this point you have more than a simple traffic violation. It has evolved into a medical aid situation. Knock on the window and attempt to get her attention. Wave your hand in front of the windshield; check for doors that are unlocked. Conduct a record check of the license plate and send an officer to the registered owner's house to gather more information. Perhaps she is in need of medication or a caretaker is able to communicate with her. If none of these options are successful, utilize a Slim Jim to open the vehicle.

Follow-up: You are now not only concerned about the woman's ability to safely operate a motor vehicle, but you are also concerned about her well-being. Another officer is calling for backup and no one is answering up. What do you have (an infraction?) and what do you do?

Obviously, the safety of the officer is more important than an infraction, and, under normal circumstances, I would respond to his call for assistance. However, in this situation, I have developed a special relationship with this female, and have a responsibility for her safety. I would remain with her until it is resolved.

Would you search the elderly female's car? The obvious answer is "no," but you should be thinking deeper. For example, is she in need of medication that is in the car? Is there a contact number in the glove compartment? If you can articulate options to the panel they will be impressed.

You are a new officer at an agency and you find out that one of your buddies from high school has applied with your agency. You know some things about the applicant that would be disqualifying. Should you volunteer the information, or wait until you are contacted by backgrounds? What if you are not contacted?

I would contact a background investigator and advise him or her of what I know. It is important that we hire only the best in police work and bringing on a substandard employee may result in consequences to the hiring agency and there could be ramifications to law enforcement in general if the background issues were serious enough.

You are off duty in a fast food restaurant standing in line when a man in front of you starts berating the cashier with racial slurs. The cashier is very upset and the manager is asking the patron to leave. He refuses and threatens to hit them if they do not serve him. What action will you take?

Be an excellent witness and call the local police. Do not intercede unless violence is imminent and someone will be seriously injured. If you do take action due to a violent situation, identify yourself as a police officer and ensure all officer safety procedures are maintained.

You are off duty driving your personal vehicle when you notice one vehicle chasing another vehicle. Both vehicles are speeding, driving erratically and nearly causing collisions. At the stop light the drivers are yelling obscenities at each other and one throws a water bottle and hits the other vehicle. The light turns green and the chase continues. What would you do?

Call the local police department and report the incident. Provide vehicle descriptions, direction of travel, etc. Do not chase them and become part of the problem.

Follow-up: You drive a few miles and see the same two drivers out of their vehicles squaring off like they are going to fight.

Do not intercede unless violence is imminent. You may pull over and observe the incident, reporting what you see to the police.

Follow-up: One driver opens his trunk and removes a crow bar and slowly approaches the other driver.

My take on this is neither one of them really want to fight or it would have happened already. They simply want to save face and I may only have to yell, "the police are on the way" for them to scurry away without resorting to violence. If they fail to leave and continue to fight, the situation has now escalated to the point of identifying myself and ordering the crow bar to be placed on the ground.

You respond to a call of a male on the ledge of the freeway overpass. When you arrive he advises you not to come any closer or he will jump. How would you handle this situation?

First establish communication and rapport with the subject. Have CHP stop traffic and contact the fire department for a ladder, and to have the paramedics standing by in case he does jump. Attempt to locate the family of the jumper and ascertain medical status, medication, mental status, and phone number of his doctor. Delegate another officer to speak with his doctor for additional information which may assist in a positive conclusion. After talking him into surrender detain him for a psychological evaluation.

Follow-up: The brother thinks he can talk him down and offers to bring this situation to a safe conclusion.

Absolutely not; you are the professional and the reason for the suicidal act could be the brother. Despite the family's good intention they may say something that sets the jumper off. To save the department from liability you should keep the brother and family informed and relay pertinent information the negotiator may have concerning the subject.

You are on patrol and you hear several shots from a high school, as you get closer to the school you hear gunshots every 4 or 5 seconds. What action will you take?

Broadcast what I hear and advise of the exact location and request immediate assistance. I would then formulate an immediate plan as, more than likely, there is an active shooter killing students. I would proceed with other officers toward the shooting in a systematic type search looking for the shooter(s); advise dispatch on the radio of my location to avoid any crossfire by other officers and to expedite any medical assistance that may become necessary.

The answers for an active shooter will be basically the same. Assess the situation quickly. Direct wounded people to a staging area and advise dispatch of the location of the wounded. They will be sending paramedics to render treatment. Ask witnesses what is happening; get descriptions of subjects, the type of weaponry, and the last known location of shooters. Information will need to be gathered fast as people are being killed, but you balance knowledge against foolishness. Call in resources, canines, helicopters, SWAT, backup, etc. Wait for the first and/or second backup officer to arrive and rapidly proceed to the sound of gunfire. Be prepared to stop the threat, most likely by shooting it. Be aware of a secondary gunman and/or bombs.

Follow-up: Would you go in alone?

I would if backup is a distance away. I do realize I could be part of the problem, but there are people that need me in there. I may take a different tactic if I was alone; possibly taking an indirect route to the sound of the gunfire, and I would also advise dispatch so other officers would be aware of my location.

You make a traffic stop on an elderly gentleman for a minor traffic violation. He cracks his window, the doors are locked, and he is not responding to questions or commands. What action will you take?

If a supervisor is requested, none will be available. Conduct a record check of the license plate and send someone to the registered owner's address to find out if there is a medical condition. Look for stickers on the vehicle that denote information such as a senior citizen park or business organizations he may be involved with. Look inside the vehicle for any other clues to resolve the situation. Look and see if he is wearing a medical bracelet. Obtain a Slim Jim and attempt to gain entry into the vehicle. Continuously consider new options to further develop your problem solving abilities.

You have been a Police Officer for six months and are attending a party with old friends. You smell an odor of Marijuana and discover several of your old friends are on the back patio passing around a joint. What will you do?

The answers will vary as this is a very real event for many officers. Speaking with the owner of the residence and stating that this is unacceptable is one way to handle the situation. The most common method is to leave immediately and advise the owner at a later time that you cannot and will not be near illegal activity. The panel will look for any ethical problems and judge your actions when faced with this situation. For example, a bad answer would be: "I would go into the house and ignore it."

You discover your partner has a seventeen-year-old girlfriend and he disclosed to you that they had sexual intercourse over the weekend. What will you do?

Possible answers include discussing the legal and moral issues with your partner and advising him to go to a supervisor with you regarding the issue. At the very minimum you must notify a supervisor and be prepared to go to Internal Affairs and testify about what was disclosed to him/her.

Do you know the difference between a civil and criminal situation?

Yes, a criminal situation is one in which a person can be arrested and charged with a specific penal code violation. A civil situation is one which can only be remedied through systems other than criminal, and the person cannot be charged with a crime.

An officer from another city is possibly involved in a car accident; he is seated on the curb approximately a hundred feet from the scene and it appears he is under the influence of alcohol.

First, advise a supervisor and then check the off duty officer for any medical injuries. Look to see what or who he may have collided with. Once it is determined that there are no injuries you will attempt to place him behind the wheel. Was there damage to the windshield and corresponding damage to the officer's face and/or head? Were there other pieces of evidence that indicated he was the driver? Did you simply ask him if he was the driver? Administer the field sobriety test to determine if the officer was driving under the influence of alcohol; if he was under the influence of alcohol he must be arrested. It is the right thing to do and any favor would be against policy and personal ethics.

You are working in the jail and you observe an inmate spit on a correctional officer and you see the correctional officer explode physically with fists and kicks. What do you do?

First, ensure the use of force is not necessary to stop an attack that you are not aware of due to the angle you are viewing from. Where are the inmate's hands? Does he have a weapon? Was he attacking the officer? If none of these factors are present or the force utilized is excessive, stop it immediately. Separate the correctional officer from the situation and secure the inmate. Call a supervisor and advise him/her of the situation.

You and another officer are interviewing a child molester at the station. Your partner is about to mentally lose it. What do you do? What would you do if you observed excessive force?

Is the officer performing an act (you would know that by preparation and a plan)? If actually real and spontaneous, you would step in and calm the situation by saying simply "let me handle this for a while." Not only would getting physical be a violation of the suspect's constitutional rights, it would also jeopardize the important case you are working on.

What do you think makes a good police officer, probation officer, firefighter, correctional officer, etc.? And how would you go about being one?

Selflessness is the most important attribute of any public servant. A good heart is vital to all of these occupations and guides them through the difficult times. A person who tries to do the right thing at all times regardless of the consequences.

Have you ever done anything you're ashamed of, and what did you learn from it?

Yes, I should have given better effort in high school. I could have been a straight "A" student. I learned never to give less than 100% and that is how I live my life now.

What do you regret most and what would you have done differently if you could?

Probably not doing my best in high school. I fully realize now the opportunities I missed and how much easier the road would have been if I had studied harder.

Alternative answer: My biggest regret is not going straight to college from high school. If I would have done so I would have received a degree by the age of twenty two instead of twenty six. On the other hand, I would not have had the work and life experience that I have now acquired through previous employment opportunities.

Do no bad mouth your previous employers. There is no upside to this tactic. There is a strong urge to trash your current or previous agency; after all it can't all be roses, you're trying to leave. Never say anything negative about where you worked or have worked. There is absolutely no upside to it. Vent to the wife, kids, cat and dog, but no one else.

What would you change about your current workplace?

This is a great question and if handled without any negativity, can help you act the interview. Offer something that you have tried to implement, but be gracious about their failure to make the change; i.e. budget, timing, etc.

Ethical Dilemmas
Remember: stop, solve, and report (SSR).
The basic formula for any question regarding ethics is to stop any illegal, unethical, or any behavior out of policy immediately. Do it publicly and with conviction if necessary. Solve the issue at hand. This book is not to teach you to regurgitate information. We expect you to learn from it and begin to understand the complexities involved in any law enforcement position. You may even disagree with the answers in the book, and that is exactly what we're looking for. When you have achieved an understanding and are able to formulate logical sequences and solutions then state them in an understandable fashion; you will be ready to join our world.

Ensure all parties are safe and then report it to a supervisor. Be totally honest with everyone involved and be clear that your intentions are to do what is right.

You are in the roll call room waiting for briefing. You hear a male officer make derogatory remarks of a sexual nature about a female coworker. What would you do?

First, I would stop the behavior. It is inappropriate at the very least and most likely a violation of policy on sexual harassment. Failure to act could result in the creation of a hostile work environment and cost the agency a large monetary sum if not dealt with. Also, it is the right thing to do to stop these derogatory comments. I would advise the involved parties I would be reporting this to a supervisor immediately. I would do this for several reasons; the situation needs to be investigated, the involved parties may have prior acts of sexual harassment, and there may have been a third party that was offended. At the very minimum, all parties involved will know where I and the department stands when it comes to ethics.

To ace this question, you must understand what sexual harassment is: it is divided into two areas, quid pro quo and a hostile work environment. Quid pro quo is a "this is that" situation. "I will give you the promotion, but you must have sex with me first." A hostile work environment is usually created over a series of events and elapsed time. On most occasions it could have been stopped at many different points. Most organizations adhere to a zero tolerance policy to any participant, including third party personnel, which means anyone who sees or hears any sexual harassment should take immediate action.

Does the answer change if you are simply walking by the conversation in the hallway?

No, not only can a third party be offended, but it is wrong and needs to be dealt with.

You are in a restaurant and your partner asks several inappropriate sexual questions to the waitress. What would you do?

I would ask him to stop after the first inappropriate remark. I would then discuss the incident with him or her after the waitress was out of ear shot. One option would be for my partner to apologize to the waitress, but I am not sure if that is the best thing to do in case of subsequent litigation. Now, I understand that this situation does not fall under the federal guidelines of sexual harassment; quid pro quo or hostile work environment, but at the very least it is inappropriate. behavior, and most likely a violation of department policy. I would immediately notify a supervisor for two reasons. First, how to deal with the situation at hand, and whether or not to address it, or to apologize to the waitress. Second, the officer may have a continuing problem with this type of behavior that I am unaware of, and if so, it needs to be addressed.

You are in court testifying on a criminal case. You hear shots from an adjoining courtroom. What will you do?

Once again, the panel wants to hear your thought process. There are numerous ways to handle this situation, and as long as they make sense you will do well in the interview. Is there a bailiff in your courtroom? Is there any emergency broadcast coming from the bailiff's radio? Can you and other law enforcement officers who happen to be in the courtroom that day observe from a back entrance? What if you see the shooter has a gun to someone's head? If you have a clear shot at the back of the gunman's head from three feet away would you shoot? These are just a few considerations. Think of three more!

You are off duty walking through a mall with your family when you hear several shots from a high powered rifle. You see people running toward you, some screaming and some bleeding. What will you do?

Unfortunately, mall shootings are not uncommon. Secure your family through a side door at the nearest business; ensure their safety first and have them call 911 to notify dispatch that you are in the mall and will be attempting to stop the shooter. It may seem foolish to not call 911 yourself, but every second is crucial, and consider that every shot you hear is someone dying tactically. Approach where the shots are being fired from, and attempt to take out the shooter. Be aware that he or she may not be alone and could also have planted explosives which unfortunately is not uncommon. He may also be wearing a vest, so don't assume he is dead if you shoot him. After the situation is controlled Call 911 and advise police and fire of the situation and the numbers and location of wounded individuals. Identify yourself to security in the mall and order them to evacuate the mall except for the wounded that cannot be moved.

You pull over a vehicle for swerving across several lanes of traffic. The driver identifies himself as a police sergeant from a neighboring city. What would you do?

This needs to be handled "by the book" for a lot of reasons. The sergeant may have an alcohol problem and if it is not addressed could lead to hurting someone in the near future. If I allowed him to leave I would be compromising my ethics as well as departmental policies. We should be held to the same standards we hold the public to. I would call my supervisor and, of course, display the utmost respect to the sergeant from the other agency. Quite possibly the field sobriety tests would be conducted at the station, out of the public eye.

What if your sergeant tells you "Officer, I'll take over," and then lets the sergeant go?

My sergeant is my superior, and I am going to believe he had a good reason to do what he did. Perhaps the other sergeant was just driving tired, or was on some type of medication I wasn't aware of. I would go back into service and respond to other emergencies.

You witness a hit and run and the driver pulls into the driveway of a large house. As you drive your police unit to the house, he runs into the residence and it appears there is a wedding party going on. What will do you do?

I am not going to chase him inside without backup. It is just too dangerous. Even if I had another officer with me, I would consider all of the factors, such as the type of party. I legally have the right to go into the house due to fresh pursuit, exigent circumstances, and the destruction of evidence (dissipating blood alcohol content) if he is under the influence of alcohol. However, is it worth it to ruin the memories of everyone at the party by barging into the house? I can simply knock on the door and ask the owner to send the driver out to me. If not I may simply tow the car and file a report with the driver's description.

You follow a biker gang of six bikes onto the freeway. Two split off and exit the off-ramp. Who do you follow and why?

Learn the biker gangs in your beat and their specific colors

Well, this is a difficult question. The bikes pulling off may be decoys or they may be the bikes with drugs and guns. I would follow the subject who had committed the most egregious violation thus far and radio the direction of travel, description, and license plates of the other to the CHP. I would activate my lights and siren and initiate a traffic stop. Because of the gang membership, I would not approach them until backup arrives; then follow them procedures of patting down and securing dangerous individuals. Write them a citation for any violations that I observed and run a warrant check for any outstanding warrants.

What if one of them gets off the motorcycle and runs into a wooded area?

I would radio the description and direction of travel and stay with the subject that stayed behind. I would be aware that the other biker could be coming around for an ambush. I would wait for my emergency backup before approaching the remaining bikers.

You are dispatched to a domestic violence situation and there is a man in the back bedroom holding his wife and child at knife point, what would you do?

The panel isn't looking for you to be an expert in police tactics; what they are looking for is to see how you think under pressure and how logical you are. First, you need to understand that these situations are real and they happen all the time and these questions are not unreasonable. It's easy to solve this crisis situation if you go step by step. To develop a public safety mindset, begin thinking what you would actually do. This will assist you in handling unbelievably chaotic situations.

The first thing you would do is call for backup, then paramedics to standby in case of an injury. You would attempt to establish rapport with the suspect and engage him in conversation and possibly call for a hostage negotiator. Keep a safe distance, do not place yourself in danger or increase the danger to the hostages. To shoot or not to shoot is a personal question that may change with each variable you're given, but you need to be prepared to shoot the suspect in order to stop the threat. Are there other means of lesser force that would solve the problem? Such as a taser or a bean bag weapon? Continue to evolve with the problem and be creative; ask dispatch to run a check of the address or the suspect's name if you know it. Does he have a history of mental illness or a primary care physician who could be called? Is he on medication that we can get him to take or trick him into taking? You will on occasion need to use force; do not be hesitant when you do, use it decisively and effectively and the situation will be resolved.

You stop a vehicle for running a red light, and as you approach the car you realize it is your mother. What would you do?

This is a tricky question for some applicants. They are torn by what they would actually do and what they believe the oral panel wants to hear. The answer should be what you would actually do. Tell your mother the consequences of running a red light and the people she can hurt driving recklessly, give her a stern warning and tell her goodbye. Believe it or not, there are some applicants who say they would give their mother a ticket, which means they are either lying, or have had a bad childhood. These applications would have trouble in the psychological examination, or are trying to placate the oral panel.

You are on duty and step into a corner market for refreshment. When you attempt to leave, three large intoxicated males step in front of the door and advise you to exit through the rear door or you're going to get hurt.

Directions to the panel will look like this: If the applicant requests backup the radio is inoperative, if the applicant uses a phone it is also inoperative. He or she should attempt to explain the consequences to the males if they do not allow him/her to pass. If the applicant uses outstanding verbal skills and good explanations, let him/her through. If the applicant is weak in his or her verbal skills keep the males at the door. Ultimately the officer will have to leave through the rear door and return with additional officers to arrest them for obstructing an officer (see if they use logic and common sense). A poor answer would be to pull his or her handgun!

You and your partner are on a call at the grocery mart. Your partner is engaged in conversation with the owner and the owner makes a few derogatory remarks against the chief of police. You overhear your partner say, "I think it's time for the chief to go." What do you do?

Tactfully interrupt the conversation and finish the call. After you and your partner are away from any citizens tell him that his comment about the chief was not only unprofessional, but also disrespectful to his boss, whom he is representing.

You respond to a child custody issue involving a male police department employee. The female advises you everything is fine, but you see red marks on her wrists and she is crying. What will you do?

You may not know all the laws, but you should always strive to "do the right thing." The right thing here would be to find out if spousal abuse is occurring. Handle with sensitivity and the respect you would on every call. Notify a sergeant as soon as you determine there is a police department employee involved. There may be ongoing investigations you are not aware of with this employee.

You are on duty in full uniform and walk into a pool hall bar/restaurant to use the restroom. On your way out a large male biker steps in front of the doorway, blocking your path and tells you the only way for you to get out is through the back window. He is holing a pool cue and seems confident in his actions.

First thing's first—initiate a friendly conversation and attempt to gain voluntary compliance, and while doing this, assess whether or not he is armed (including the pool cue), has friends with him, and has any physical weaknesses in case of an attack. Use your radio to call for backup, but the panel will tell you it's inoperative. You should adapt and use all available resources, such as the business phone, cell phone, or even request to use another customer's phone.

Follow-up: You continue to converse with the subject and he still refuses to move. What will you do?

Some applicants pull their handgun and then they are stuck. How long do you point a weapon at someone before you finally decide to put it back in your holster? News flash: not everyone complies with your orders, even when you're pointing a gun at them. Will you try and take him on physically? How big are you? How big is he? Does he have any martial arts training? Do you have any martial arts training? If you do, will your training protect you against an attack with multiple assailants while you're grappling with this subject? Begin thinking about these types of situations and truly understand your personal skills and abilities.

This is a difficult situation in which you may be forced to swallow your pride. You may very well crawl out the window and come back with the rest of the shift. Ultimately you'll return, arrest this subject, and win this encounter. We always win, we have to win...

What do we mean "we have to win"?
"I must handle the situation within the law and arrest this individual for obstruction of a police officer. He interfered with the performance of my duties and will stand trial for it. I will not use force unless necessary, but he will go to jail."

Firefighter Oral Interview Tips

Even if you are not interested in this particular profession, answer the questions using logic as your guide. The broader your knowledge the better you will do in your respective interview.

I spoke with Fire Captain Stephen Homer, who is a veteran firefighter with the Santa Ana Fire Department. He has interviewed over a thousand prospective firefighters. His advice is simple yet powerful: look sharp and be prepared with a good opening and closing statement. Smile and speak to the panel. Do your best to connect with them. Understand the culture of the agency you are testing for. You should have visited their facilities prior to the interview and should be able to explain what impressed you and why you would be good for the department.

If you did your homework, which should include law enforcement preparation, the board will see everything they want in a candidate right in front of them! The most common problem if the candidate thinking that they already have the job and showing up unprepared. Also, the better prepared you are the less nervous you will be.

Firefighter

Firefighter Oral Situational Questions

You are in the fire station and you see a six pack of beer with one missing in the refrigerator. What will you do?

You may feel this is a trick and opt to report it to a supervisor and your chain of command immediately. This is not a good answer as you haven't researched or inquired about anything. Go step by step and the situation will most likely be resolved with a logical explanation. First, look around. Is the beer being used in cooking? You may hear someone talk about the beer that added flavor to the stew they made last night. Don't jump to conclusions and think about the likelihood of a fellow firefighter risking his career to drink on duty. And, consider that if he had such a problem, would there be five beers left in the refrigerator?

If you cannot figure it out, ask someone and you may get such a simple explanation that you'll laugh at what you feared. However, if a fellow firefighter *is* drinking on duty he is placing a huge amount of liability on himself, the department, and his co-workers. The panel may ask you "what if the supervisor told you to mind your own business and keep your mouth shut?" At this point you must go above him in your chain of command and explain the situation. You may be treated like a pariah by other firefighters, but your ethical standards will be well known throughout the department.

While your partner is performing a medical aid, you witness a mistake of medical procedures. This caused obvious medical discomfort to the patient. What would you do?

Ask your partner what happened first. There are many things that won't make sense until you hear the explanation or gain enough experience to understand what occurred. Not assuming your partner did something wrong will foster a good working relationship through which you can both improve your skills. If your partner did do something wrong and it caused medical problems or liability to the department you and he should speak with your supervisor to let him or her know what happened. This will give your supervisor the opportunity to mitigate any issues that have come up during this situation that you may not be aware of. It may encourage additional training at the department that would benefit both the department and community.

You are an off-duty firefighter eating at a restaurant with your family. You notice it is overcrowded and the rear exit is chained and locked shut. What would you say or do, if anything?

You are sworn to protect the public, and this situation is definitely a danger to their safety. Contact the manager and advise of your concern as a private citizen and customer. Perhaps the manager has a perfectly good explanation such as, they are working on the underground electrical lines directly outside of this exit ("We are using the alternate exit through the kitchen, and it has been approved by the fire chief"). If the manager gets argumentative with you, which is highly unlikely, identify yourself and tell him he needs to correct this fire hazard immediately, and then follow-up with inspectors the next day. You need to protect the people even if you will be despised.

You are a firefighter and are on the scene of a medical aid and you see your captain involved in a physical altercation. The police are en route to the scene code three. You understand if you get involved you may lose your position as a reserve firefighter. What would you say or do, if anything?

Your captain is obviously in danger and you must do what you can to assist him. You do not have the time to ask the captain why he is involved with the subject. Your trust in him and his position tells you he is doing the right thing.

Note: You should be able to answer any questions involving the acronyms for fire and the nomenclature of each particular acronym.

Police Dispatcher

Dispatcher Oral Interview Tips

Be prepared to listen to a radio broadcast and take notes. Pay particular attention to the location, description of suspects and vehicles, and the type of crime, as well as the weapons involved. Be able to give directions to the scene of the crime using North, South, East and West.

Parking Control Officer

Once again, even if you are not interested in this particular profession, answer the questions anyway using logic as your guide.

Parking Control Officer Oral Situational Questions
You are assigned to a parking problem in an upper class part of town. You are writing parking tickets and several residents come out of their houses and state that your vehicle is double parked and demand that you write yourself a ticket. What do you do?

Call a supervisor immediately. Continue to do your job and maintain professional decorum. Watch for safety issues as irate people are not thinking properly and may attack. If it becomes too hostile drive away and return with the supervisor. Public safety officials are exempt from parking violations while performing their jobs. This does mean the privilege can be abused and in this case it wasn't. If I finished writing the tickets before the supervisor arrived I would leave and ask him or her to meet me at another location where I could explain what occurred.

You write a handicap violation and begin to walk away. You hear and old lady trying to get your attention. "Officer, I don't have my handicap placard yet, but I have the paperwork in the glove compartment." She hobbles to the passenger door in pain and appears to have permanent injury by the way she walks. How would you respond?

I will be making a judgment based on the spirit of the law versus the letter of the law in this case. If she does have the paperwork indicating the placard is in progress I will void the citation. I would then advise my supervisor.

Follow-up: What if she does not have the paperwork, but it is still apparent that she is disabled?

Well, first I will have to believe it is her vehicle and she actually drove to the location. I know a handicap violation is expensive and it could be she was actually a passenger and assisting the driver in evading the fine. This would seem to be an unusual situation where I would need to contact my supervisor. I would advise him or her that it appears a disabled elderly woman is in the process of obtaining a handicap placard and request to void the citation. If I could not get in contact with the supervisor I would advise on procedures to challenge the ticket.

You are towing a vehicle that violated a registration law and the owner shows up with the paperwork that proves his registration is up to date. The only problem is the tow truck has already hooked up the vehicle and is now entitled, by law, to a $60.00 drop fee. What would you do?

Though it was legal to tow the vehicle, new information proved the registration to be valid. The right thing to do would be to drop the vehicle and request that the tow company waive the fees. If they refuse, contact a supervisor and explain the situation and see if he or she can offer some advice. If contact with a supervisor is not available and the tow company still refuses to waive the fee, explain the situation to the owner of the vehicle and see if he will pay the drop fee. If that does not work, sign for the drop fee on behalf of the city and write a report explaining the situation.

Police Service Officer Oral Situational Questions

You are transcribing a police report from a tape recorder. The report is going along fine until a conversation in the background was unintentionally recorded. The conversation is between two officers, with one asking the other to stretch the truth on his report so they can "put this animal away." What would you do?

This is out of your league and you want to bring it to the attention of your immediate supervisor now. Ou are not to judge or elaborate on what you heard. If you are questioned by a sergeant or internal affairs answer the questions truthfully. It is very important to keep the information confidential and not participate in gossip.

Security Officer Oral Situational Questions

Note: If a serious offense, such as robbery, burglary, or assault with a deadly weapon has been committed, you will need help to apprehend the suspect. Call the police immediately. Even police who are trained to make forcible arrests are encouraged to call for help in dangerous situations.

You are patrolling the grounds at a factory at 2:00 a.m. and you see two armed adults entering the stock room. What should you do?

Go to a safe location where you can observe and report the incident. If there is not a safe position in which to do this, get out of the area noting as many details as possible, such as type of vehicle, license plate numbers, and any other information that will assist the police in capturing these individuals.

While you are guarding a sporting goods store, a man runs out of the store. Ten seconds later, the owner runs to you and says there has been a robbery. What should you do?

Have the owner call the police in your presence while you observe the individual and report details that will assist in leading to capture.

You are patrolling a store parking lot. A shopper loads Christmas gifts into a station wagon parked in the lot and goes back to do more shopping. The windows of the wagon are open and three boys are gathered around the vehicle peering at the gifts. What should you do?

Make your presence known. It will likely inhibit their behavior thus avoiding the theft.

You are on duty in a jewelry store. An employee showing diamond rings to a customer is called to the telephone. The customer is left alone with the display box of diamond rings. What should you do?

Once again, presence is a powerful tool for a security officer. I would be obvious in letting them know that I am watching and discouraging any criminal activity.

Loss Prevention Oral Situational Questions

How much power do loss prevention officers have in a situation involving apprehension?

They have the power to arrest within their jurisdiction, as does any citizen (the store employing them/parking lot)

What grounds must a loss prevention associate have to arrest an individual?

They must have probable cause to make an arrest, reasonable suspicion is not enough.

Does a request for an attorney obligate loss prevention associates to stop questioning or asking a suspect for additional information?

No, Miranda requirements and the right to an attorney is only if the POLICE are conducting the questioning. Loss prevention, as well as any other citizen, can question an individual and ignore any right to request an attorney be present.

What are some indicators of possible external theft?

Empty packages/wrapping, stashed merchandise, customers randomly grabbing merchandise, customers watching associates rather than the merchandise in front of them, overly filled shopping carts, customers who avoid associates, baggy clothes or extra clothing such as huge jackets that don't match the current weather conditions, carrying large bags/purses, theft markers such as hats/shoes placed to indicated stashed merchandise.

What are the 2 major categories of external thieves?

1. The professional shoplifter: Thievery is a business and because this is how they make their living, there is a possibility they will become violent when confronted. Professional shoplifters range from being highly skilled technicians to thug-like. Some professionals work in teams or use elaborate distraction scenarios. The lesser skilled professionals use force and fear much like gang intimidation and often commit grab-and-run thefts. Being a professional means that they steal merchandise for a living, and just like other trades, practice makes perfect. Intelligent professionals are very difficult to stop in a society where retail stores openly display their merchandise.

2. The amateur: Shoplifting is simply a crime of opportunity and most shoplifters are amateurs; however, there are growing numbers of organized theft rings and people who make their living by stealing from retail stores. Amateur shoplifters can be highly skilled, and some steal almost every day. Most amateurs are opportunistic, crude in their methods, and are detected more often than others.

What are some examples of Internal Theft?

A cashier ringing up merchandise, voiding the sale and then pocketing the money; intentionally not ringing up merchandise for a friend or relative; improper use of employee discount; stashing merchandise in the store to be picked up by an accomplice; refund fraud.

What are some things you can do to prevent internal theft?

Look at "voided/cancelled/deleted sales report" every day. Look at "returned transactions" report every day. Keep the back door closed and alarm it, which is one of the easiest ways for employees to sneak out merchandise. Review security videos on a regular basis and most importantly, make sure your staff knows you do so.

If you do arrest an employee for stealing, let all your employees know that they did NOT get away with it! This can be an effective way to prevent theft and inventory shrinkage.

What are some important things to keep in mind when finding potential theft indicators?

Make sure to communicate the problem to management/associates as they might not be acting alone; keep an open mind and look for accomplices, use teamwork even with regular associates to even the odds against multiple thieves as you can't be everywhere at one time.

What are steps you can take to minimize the potential for a false arrest claim?
You must see the shoplifter approach the merchandise. You must see the shoplifter select the merchandise. You must see the shoplifter conceal, convert or carry away the merchandise. You must apprehend the shoplifter outside the store

What are steps you can take to avoid other related claims?

Approach from the front (so the shoplifter cannot make a false claim). Have at least one witness of the same sex present at all times. Clearly identify yourself as the store representative or security officer. State the reason for the detention and ask for the item back. Don't be afraid to immediately disengage and apologize if you make a mistake. Listen for spontaneous utterances (i.e. "I forgot to pay for it"). Closely escort the shoplifter to a private office. Do not chase the shoplifter through the store. Always be polite and professional even if the shoplifter is not. Do not use excessive force (i.e. double lock handcuffs). Do not make threats or exchange insults. Accommodate reasonable medical and handicap requests. Process the arrest swiftly according to store policy. Save, tag, and photograph the stolen merchandise as evidence. Cooperate with the police and appear in court, if necessary.

Paralegal Interview Questions

Every aspiring paralegal should research and know certain aspects of the firm he/she is applying for employment. For example, the most basic rule of thumb involves a fundamental understanding of the firm's major practice area(s), number of attorneys, and support staff employees. It is important for a paralegal to know the firm's reputation in the legal community, if the firm employs high quality attorneys with strong academic backgrounds, senior level/partners vs. associates/mid level attorneys, and the firm's growth, stability, and profitability over the past 10-15 years.

A paralegal must be well-informed on who the firm's clients are and how the firm procures new clients. This requires awareness of how the firm markets to existing clients while also attracting prospective clients, which is generally easily obtained online, through legal articles, trade publications, etc.

A paralegal is often the primary channel of communication between the firm and the client, and knowledge of the firm's background and culture enhances the paralegal's ability to communicate with the appropriate level of formality with both supervising attorneys and clients. Understanding the professional environment will help the paralegal thrive in both the hiring interview and on the job.

While many paralegal job interview questions mirror those used for other professions, a recent graduate of a paralegal studies program will certainly benefit from preparing for some of these common questions.

Why do you want to be a paralegal?

This question provides the employer insight to the individual's interest in the law as well as his/her career
aspirations in the legal field. A paralegal should answer honestly, including whether or not he/she plans on the possibility of enrolling in law school or prefers seeking promotion/advancement to a Senior/Managing Paralegal position at a large firm. This way a paralegal finds out quickly if the firm presents an ideal fit.

What is your understanding of court rules, forms, statutes, laws, and legal procedures?

Every new paralegal must understand that applicants are not expected to answer this question in the same manner as an attorney. An effective paralegal assists and supports a lawyer by possessing competent research skills, strong critical thinking skills, excellent written and verbal communication skills, proficient computer skills, and the ability to manage multiple calendaring events to ensure the meeting of deadlines critical to litigation. Therefore, a new paralegal should gravitate to an area of the law that he or she excelled in academically and facilitates his/her ability to articulate a sound response to this line of questioning.

How has your paralegal education prepared you for employment in the field?

This is an opportunity for the paralegal to expound upon his or her coursework, especially detailing specific projects and/or cases he/she worked on, including specific assignments/tasks/duties that demonstrate competency in the subject matter as well as strong analytical ability. It is helpful if the paralegal mentions the high level of interaction with attorney instructors as that demonstrates an understanding of the profession and the ability to follow directions and complete tasks with little or no supervision. Firms want to feel confident that the candidate possesses the requisite level of preparedness for the position.

Tell me about a time you interacted with a difficult client.

As mentioned earlier, this is a very important question. It is common practice for attorneys to be unavailable to talk to clients when they are in court and preparing for court dates, hearings, trials, etc. and the paralegal is required to handle general client inquiries. A paralegal is required to possess a high level of professionalism, integrity, and empathy for the client's case and a good demeanor, patience, and excellent verbal skills. A candidate should point to specific examples that demonstrate his/her ability to adapt to various personalities. Previous customer service experience is very helpful. The candidate should also express the importance of documenting every time he/she communicates with a client.

Social Worker Oral Interview Question
What skills do you have to make you an effective social worker?

I have good communication both written and orally, good organizational skills (with examples), an ability to critically reflect my practice and good interpersonal skills in engaging with professionals and service users and the maturity not to personalize issues of conflict.

Child Protection Services Oral Situational Questions

You receive a call from a distressed grandmother who isn't able to get her 7 year old grandson to take his ADHD medication in the morning. Consequently, he is refusing to get dressed and refusing to go to school. She has also called the police and says she can't handle him anymore. She insists that he be put into care, because she can't deal with him anymore.

A. Tell the grandmother to be more firm and strict with her grandson, and show him who is boss

B. Consult with supervisor, and make preparations to take child into care

C. Laugh at the grandmother's inability to control her grandmother and ask her to stop wasting the agency's time

D. Ask police to help brace the child while grandmother administers the medication

E. Try to reason with the boy to get him to take his medication

Answer : B

The fundamental job of a child protection worker is to

A. Strengthen the community
B. Helping parents improve core parenting skills
C. Protect rights and safety of children
D. Prepare legal documents for court proceedings
E. Remove children from homes that are unsafe

Answer : C

Child Protection Workers should spend the majority of their time:

A. Completing and updating government mandated child and family assessments and profiles

B. Consulting with the supervisor regarding plan of action for families

C. Attending family court proceedings to represent child in court

D. Making home visits to assess child safety and provide support

E. Meet with team members to provide support and encouragement

Answer: D

You have been assigned to work with a family because of allegations made that the mother has been hitting the 12 year old son. There are two younger children in the home (ages 5 and 10). The allegations were made by the 12 year old at school, when asked about a bruise on his shoulder and back. You go to the address provided for the family by the school and knock on the door. You see movement in the window and the car in the driveway, but nobody answers, what do you do?

A. Begin threatening the mother that the police will arrest her if she doesn't answer.

B. Break down the door and enter the home.

C. Document your attempt, notify your supervisor and consult about the next step

D. Call the police to break down the door

E. Close the file, she obviously doesn't want to talk to you anyway.

Answer : C

Before apprehending a child, you should always:

A. Consult with your supervisor(s) to ensure just cause for apprehension

B. Make sure you have enough gas in your tank to get all the way back to the agency.

C. Ask the parents if that is okay with them.

D. Ask the child if they want to be apprehended.

E. See if any neighbors can take the child while you figure out what to do with the family

Answer : A

Your agency receives a call about a possible neglect of a new born baby (approximately 3 weeks old). The anonymous caller states the mother and father are often seen in the back yard smoking marijuana while the baby can be heard crying in the home, sometimes for hours. How soon does your agency need to respond?

A. 24 hours
B. 48 hours
C. 1 week
D. By the end of the month

Answer : A

You are called to investigate a two parent family with 3 children, ages 12, 6, and 18 months. It has been alleged that the father is physically abusing the mother and the children are not being fed or clothed for school appropriately. The school has called that the 12 and 6 year old do not have adequate lunches and wear dirty clothing. What/who is the most urgent need in this family?

A. Anger management courses for the father

B. Financial support for the family to supply appropriate food and clothing for the school children

C. The comprehensive needs of the 18 month old child, then the older children

D. Counseling for the mother

E. Criminal charges for the father and removal of him from the home (arrest)

Answer : C

You've just finished a very busy week at work, its now Saturday and you're in the grocery store for the weekly grocery shopping trip. As you fill your cart with the last item (chocolate mint ice cream) you hear a scream from behind you. You turn around to see a toddler getting slapped by her mother and being told to shut up. When the child keeps crying, the mother slaps the child again. You are obligated to:

A. Do nothing, you're not on duty, time to check out and get home so you can eat some ice cream

B. Call the police and leave as quickly as possible

C. Call the after hours hotline at the agency for direction on making a referral or to call the police

D. Hit the mother and ask how she likes it

E. Show the mother your badge and threaten her to stop it or else

Answer : C

You get a call from a child who claims his mother has kicked him out of the house and he wants to have your agency take him into the agency's care. Upon finding out his birth date, you find he is 18 years old. What is your best option?

A. Take the young man into your agency care in foster or group home placement

B. Tell him to find a comfortable box

C. Refer him to the local shelter

D. Refer him and his family to family counseling services

E. Refer him to various social service programs for youth, after conducting an investigation to determine if any children under 16 are at risk of abandonment, abuse or neglect in the home.

Answer : E

You and your fellow team member are assigned to investigate a family suspected of abusing the two children. As you conduct you're assessment, you find that the abuse happened by the children's father who does not live in the home. The chidren's mother has been trying to find work to afford to move to new home. After completing your assessment you decide the children should stay with their mother and you begin to think of ways to support her with her plans to find work and move. Your team member tells you he thinks the children should be apprehended because they aren't safe there. What is your response?

A. Call your supervisor, voice your opinion, support the final decision made by supervisor.

B. Argue with the team member until he bends, you're obviously right

C. Tell him if he wants to apprehend, he'll have to do it alone, then leave.

D. Agree with his decision, to avoid an argument, then complain about it to the supervisor when you get back

E. Agree with this decision, and then worry about whether it was right the whole next week while on vacation

Answer : A

As a child protection worker, you work in a team of six workers with a supervisor and a team assistant. New files are assigned based on case load and worker fit. Because your supervisor believes you can handle it, she assigns eight new files to you which will put you three files over the cap set by the organization. You should:

A. Be grateful you have a job and get to work

B. Take on the files and then vent to other team members about the work load

C. Decline the new files on the spot

D. Approach your supervisor alone and voice your objective concerns about the work load exceeding your limit

E. Go over your supervisors head, because she obviously doesn't understand your needs, and speak to the unit manager about the policy violation

Answer : D

The best way to get work done is to:

A. Skip lunches

B. Work late

C. Take work home

D. Come in early

E. Work hard during the business hours, then go home and recharge your batteries

Answer : E

You notice you've been coming in early, skipping lunches and staying late more often. You've also been taking files home to work on them. While you used to enjoy going to the gym to exercise, you haven't had time lately. This is a sign that you:

A. Are a dedicated worker and should keep it up.

B. Are working hard, and deserve a raise

C. Should take a vacation

D. Are beginning to burn out and should make immediate changes to your schedule to restore balance in your own life

E. Love being a child protection worker

Answer : D

Why do you want to be a child protection worker?

A. I hate people that abuse children. I want to take their children away so they can't hurt them anymore

B. I had a difficult childhood and helping other children helps me feel better about myself, almost making up for what happened to me

C. I believe in the intrinsic value of all people and want to help make children safe and happy, and help families improve coping strategies.

D. The pay is right what I need coming out of school.

Answer : C

After apprehending a child, you should place the child with:

A. Who they choose to be placed with
B. Their other parent (if separated)
C. Their grandparents
D. A foster home
E. An agency designated safe home that has been pre-approved by the

agency, whether it be family, foster or friend

Answer : E

Animal Control Interview Questions

What are your thoughts on euthanasia?

In this case, the best answer to get the job is going to be, "I think that it's unfortunate there are not enough people out there adopting animals and that euthanasia is a sad, but necessary, thing we have to do for population control and to keep the shelters from becoming over-crowded." However, if you truly feel against euthanasia and still want the job, try: "I'm really against euthanasia and am willing to spend extra time trying to get animals adopted quicker." You may not get the job, but at least you've shown initiative and didn't lie about your true feelings.

Why do you want to work for Animal Control?

I want to be an advocate for animals and to educate people about how to care for animals.

Phlebotomist Situational Questions

You run across medical information about someone you know, how would you handle getting home at night and possibly wanting to talk about that to my husband

I wouldn't have wanted someone running across my information and speaking to their significant other, so I respected the privacy of others.

How have you handled conflict in the workplace?

They are looking for "I tried to handle the problem, and if that didn't work I would bring management in"

How would you react in a situation where you had to perform a blood draw and the patient's family was a different culture than your own?

where I used to work, I ran across this situation frequently and one of the ways I handled it was to always smile at the people, utilize their family as translators if possible, make sure my body language is relaxed so they won't become perturbed, etc.

Why do you want to go from your current position to one where you make less money

It's not about the money for me, It's about having a satisfying low stress job.

Internal Revenue Agent Situational Question

As an IRS Revenue Agent, how would you procede if one of your friends have $50,000 to invest in a company that you know is not a profitable business and asks your advice?

I would say that I can't give him advice about that company and still maintain my professional integrity

Court Reporter Interview Questions

Describe your work experience and how it qualifies you as a court stenographer.

Focus on the aspects of your experience that apply to this position. Highlight any particularly impressive accomplishments and achievements. Be sure to mention any awards or commendations you may have received.

Name some resources that could be useful to a stenographer.

Prepare a mental list of resources you have found to be useful. These can include practice dictation materials for speed building, research sites on the Internet, software programs, etc.

What experience do you have with personal computer programs?
Talk about the software you've worked on and what you've done with these programs. Be sure to mention any measurable competencies

Give us an example of your ability to work under pressure and deadlines?

Think of a time when you performed above and beyond the call of duty, under the pressure of a tight deadline. Tell how you remained calm and devoted whatever time was necessary to accomplish the task, within the time allotted.

How should you handle a witness that is scheduled for a court appearance and does not show up to testify?

Discuss how you would work with your client (attorney, judge, etc.) to schedule another time to record the testimony. The main point here is that you should demonstrate that you are able to handle unforeseen circumstances. Life isn't always convenient and you need be flexible.

How should you handle a witness that is scheduled for a court appearance and does not show up to testify?

Discuss how you would work with your client (attorney, judge, etc.) to schedule another time to record the testimony. The main point here is that you should demonstrate that you are able to handle unforeseen circumstances. Life isn't always convenient and you need be flexible.

What should you do if you were transcribing another stenographer's notes and could not read them?

Use this question to highlight your ability to solve problems in a positive way, without offending your colleagues.

Do you work more effectively in a team environment or by yourself? Why?

This is a tricky question. You will need to come up with an answer, which you should also support with a true life example, that will show you can do both. You want to demonstrate you have the ability to work unsupervised, and also in a collaborative environment.

Where do you see yourself in five years?

Employers don't want to spend time and money training people that will be moving on to "greener pastures" soon. Answer in a way that will give the impression you intend to improve your skills and become a valuable asset to the company for many years to come.

Domestic Violence Advocate Interview Questions

What would you say are the most important character qualities for a domestic violence advocate?

Compassion and patience are two of the most prevalent, but there are numerous possible traits depending on the applicants. The answer to this question says a lot about the applicant's line of thinking and what they view as important.

What's your experience with and/or knowledge of the criminal justice field?

This can be anything from taking a few classes, family members in law enforcement or other related fields. Do not hold back on this question, take the opportunity to tell the interviewer why you would fit this role.

Tell me about a time when you walked with someone through a difficult time in their life. What happened? How did you respond?

The interviewer is working from the principle - the best predictor of future behavior is past behavior – so expand on your answer and explain in detail what you have done for others.

Tell me about a time when you dealt with a crisis. What happened? How did you respond?

Once again the interviewer is utilizing the principle - the best predictor of future behavior is past behavior.

Unusual Questions

These are the questions you did not anticipate, which are designed to observe how quickly you think on your feet. I guarantee you will think of a better answer on your way home, but don't worry about it. Let's prepare for a few of the possible zingers.

Who was or is the greatest American?

Don't over-analyze this question. Who is it? Have justification and passion for the answer you provide. The only caveat is to stay away from current political figures. It has very little upside a huge possible downside. Here is an example: "I think the greatest American was George Washington. He succeeded in the face of incredible diversity and if not for him, we would be called something different than Americans."

Who is the best leader? Describe why you selected that person.

Your answer could be a boss, co-worker, or your parents, or maybe you decide to select a figure in history. "I believe the best leader was Abraham Lincoln. There are very few individuals that endured that much and still had such a significant impact. He brought our country together in the most difficult of times and circumstances."

Are you a leader or a follower? Explain your answer.

I am both a follower and a leader. I am extremely loyal to my superiors, but still voice a way to build a better mouse trap when the situation presents itself. Peers and supervisors give a lot of weight to my opinions which have resulted in both formal and informal leadership roles.

How would you describe yourself?

A loyal, hardworking, industrious person who gives 100% to everything I do. Note: this should be followed-up with a mini opening statement.

What are your major strengths?

Example: "Writing ability is one of my major strengths. I received an award for literary promise from the academic staff at UNLV. I also have a way of calming angry and aggressive people and resolving a situation."

What are your major weaknesses?
Example: "A major weakness is my punctuality. I am early to everything. For example, I was in the parking lot an hour before my interview today. It has definitely been brought up as a weakness by my husband, who, by the way, is always late." Smile when you say that last part. Remember, they ask you for a weakness and you give them an obvious strength.

What are your outside interests?

Be honest. They may follow-up and ask you about it. For example: "I love to read anything I can get my hands on" might provoke a question from the panel about the latest novel you've read, etc. You want to keep it real. Discuss your interests. Running, painting, yoga, etc.

Why did you leave your last job?

Again, be honest, but be careful not to bad mouth your previous employer. Be gracious and tactful. Consider a positive reason for leaving your previous employer. Was there another opportunity that was more beneficial to your career path? Was there another job that made more financial sense for you? What about your family? Did you relocate and decide to change jobs for that reason? Would your previous employer hire you back? Definitely inform that panel if that is the case.

Where you do you see yourself in five years?

Answer this question tactfully and straightforwardly. Be as truthful as you possibly can, but keep it simple. Consider your goals—both personally and professionally.

What are your goals in life? One year, five years and ten years.

Answer honestly.

What attributes do you possess that will assist you in public safety?

Tell them about your attributes. If you can learn to speak another language, including sign language, do it. For example, a nearby city has one of the largest deaf populations in the country; do you think it would be impressive if you began to learn sign language and volunteered at the School of the Deaf?

What is your favorite movie and why?

This may be a hard question to answer, but go with it. Do not worry about political correctness, but also do not choose a raunchy comedy. "My favorite movie is *Dances with Wolves*. It's a movie about a soldier learning the ways of Native-Americans and the challenges faced by people during the Civil War era."

What is the title of the last book you read and what insight did it provide?

Here's an example: "I read a book titled *CSI: Beyond the Yellow Tape*. It was outstanding because it gave practical advice on the methods a real crime scene investigator uses to do his or her job."

Crime Scene Investigators collecting evidence at a homicide.

Crime Scene Investigation Interview Questions

Note: Most of the answers parallel the answers you would give for any public safety position. Try to practice answers to each of the following straight-forward questions. Some examples will be provided.

Tell us about yourself and your background
Why do you want to be a crime scene investigator?
Why do you want to work for this specific agency?

What type of qualities does a crime scene investigator possess and do you think you possess these qualities? If so, please give us an example.

Example: Integrity is vitally important to a crime scene investigator for a variety of reasons. Testimony in court being the most crucial. Attention to detail is important to give an accurate account of the crime scene. CSI must be methodical and patient. I was a cashier at Big Five Sporting Goods and noticed the cash register was short of funds. I checked several hours of video on my own time and discovered that one of the employees was stealing money. I notified management and she was fired.

Describe two of your negative qualities.

Describe two of your positive attributes.

When collecting a piece of evidence, where on that piece of evidence would you mark it before collecting it?

This is a trick question. Listen very carefully and explain your answer. Example: I would not mark the evidence. I would place the evidence into envelopes or any device prescribed by policy. My job would be to maintain the evidence as consistently as possible.

(Situational question) If a senior crime scene investigator tells you to collect something out of protocol and you know it is against your department's policy, what should you do?

First, ask "can we do that?" and then advise the senior investigator that you know it is not the usual protocol. If they have satisfactory answer, continue processing the evidence as they wish. You could have misunderstood the procedure or misread the policy, and should rely on the experience of the senior. Look up the policy later and if it differs from what occurred, speak with the senior and then advise a supervisor together.

(Situational question) If a supervisor orders you to destroy or compromise a piece of evidence, would you do it?

No. You should advise the supervisor that not only is it a violation of policy, it is also against the law and would embarrass the police department.

Have you had any negative relationships with fellow employees in the past, and if so, how have you resolved those situations?

Do you have any questions you would like to ask the interview panel?

Note: NO! Absolutely not! You do not have questions. Do not, I repeat, do not fall for this trick. College professors train you to ask a few questions to show your interest. What questions can you ask that will make you appear more prepared? Think about that question for a while. If you have not given a closing statement, use this opportunity to close with a thank you and a promise to be an outstanding employee.

Note: The oral panel will sometimes ask you about a background issue they see on your application. You must be prepared with an answer that will get you to the next phase of the process. Utilize the first five seconds to admit to what you and the next twenty-five seconds articulating how you have corrected the issue and actually improved because of it. Almost any negative can be turned into a positive if you have taken the steps necessary to improve yourself.

We see you here on your application you were fired from XYZ Grocery Mart. What happened?

Example: Yes, I was. I was the workhorse of the stocking section. I would come in at all hours of the night; pretty much whenever they wanted me to. On one occasion I asked them for the night off three weeks in advance and it was verbally granted. I purchased tickets to a play for my mother's birthday. When the schedule came out it had me on duty that day. I spoke with my boss, the one who had previously granted my request and approved my time off, and he said "You either want the job or not. Be here or you're fired." I knew I could have called in sick, but I didn't want to lie, so I told my boss a few days later that I wouldn't be there because of the special occasion and pre-paid tickets. He fired me on the spot. I believe he will tell you I was an exceptional employee.

We noticed on your application that you have had numerous jobs and at times have failed to give two weeks notice before leaving said jobs. Why?

Example: True, in my younger years I wasn't as responsible as I should have been, and failing to give notice is evidence of that. In the last few years I have worked for two companies and left the one in good graces for a higher paying supervisor position. I am an outstanding employee, and will also be such for your organization.

I see on your application that you were fired from ABX Manufacturing. What happened?

Example: That is true. I had a punctuality problem. I was fairly treated and given a warning and then arrived late and was fired. That was over two years ago and since then I have adopted a philosophy that it is better to be one hour early than one minute late. I have been employed at XYZ electronics for the past two years and have perfect attendance and punctuality.

We see from your application that you have been arrested. What happened?

Example: Yes, I was arrested three years ago for disturbing the peace. I had too much to drink and talked back to the officer when he told us to leave. I know I was wrong and since that time have detached myself from the club and alcohol scene. I have spent my time working, going to school, and volunteering for charitable organizations. I actually spoke with Background Investigator Jones and asked if enough time had elapsed to apply for this position. He said that if there were no other issues associated with this type of behavior he would like to see me apply.

We see from your application that you have received numerous tickets. Why?

Example: I have not been the best driver. However, about three years ago I realized how dangerous driving in excess of the speed limit was, not only to myself, but also to innocent people. I can honestly say I do not drive over the speed limit now, and I truly understand the importance of this issue.

Probation Officer Situational Question

http://www.youtube.com/watch?v=RPYfq5dvxx8

CSI Situational Question

http://www.youtube.com/watch?v=h23o7eJYfgc

Chapter 5 Discussion Questions

1
- What key aspects are panel members looking for when judging your answers to situational qusetions?

2
- What are some resources available to police officers to effectively perform their job?

3
- What are some example scenario questions you might be asked and what are some acceptable answers?

4
- What is the best way to mitigate questions pertaining to issues with your background?

Chapter 6
Closing Statement

Learning Objectives

1. • Key pointers to a successful closing statement in terms of time and content

2. • Appropriate and inappropriate questions you may ask at the conclusion of your interview

3. • Proper post-interview practices and how you to approach getting feedback from the agency

Closing Statement

You will almost always be given an opportunity for a closing statement. This is your opportunity to correct any misconceptions or tie up any loose ends that may have occurred during the interview. If the panel is still unsure about passing you, a good and honest closing statement might win them over.

You want to recap your accomplishments and leave the board with a good feeling. The statement should be approximately 30 to 45 seconds long. Be careful not to ramble as you will experience what is called diminishing returns. We have all heard people speak for longer than a minute and we were bored to death. Conversely, think of someone you could listen to forever and never get bored or disinterested. Be that person!

There is a great story about a famous author that describes diminishing returns. He was in church, listening to a preacher give a sermon about why the congregation should reach deep into their pockets for some much-needed repairs to the church. After a few minutes the author was so inspired he pulled a twenty dollar bill from his wallet and was eagerly awaiting the opportunity to place it in the basket. The preacher continued to talk and he put the twenty back and pulled out a ten dollar bill. A few minutes later the preacher was still on his sermon and the author put the ten back and pulled out a couple of ones. By the time the preacher finished his sermon, the author took fifty cents out of the basket for his trouble. I see this happen all the time. An otherwise intelligent, well qualified applicant talks himself out of a job. There is an old saying which goes like this: "You already sold it, don't buy it back."

Another example of diminishing returns: imagine craving chocolate all day and finally getting a chance to eat some late in the afternoon. The first few bites will be heaven, but then you start to experience diminishing returns. Each successive bite will be a little less enjoyable. Eventually you will come to the point where the chocolate will be a negative experience.

I am spending so much on this concept because the same thing happens in the interview! Stop talking at the high point just before you begin to lose points incrementally due to diminishing returns. So…

Is there anything you would like to add?

"I would like to thank the panel for your time and if honored with selection I will finish #1 in the academy and do my best to uphold the outstanding reputation of the department. Thank you."

Questioning the Questioners

Do not ask any questions during the process despite what many college or university professors or advisors tell you. If you feel you must ask a question for whatever reason, ensure that it pertains directly to the process, such as: what is the next step should I be successful? Other personal questions will backfire. In fact, be careful what questions you ask at anytime. You may believe it is an informal setting only to find differently later. The old saying "there is no such thing as a stupid question" is not true, and is in reality a stupid slogan. Of course there are stupid questions and stupid questions are very good indicators of you level of intelligence. If you're wondering what you need to do and want to ask a question, wait until the end as the speak may answer the questions during the lecture, or, more likely, some other unsuccessful application will ask the question and be the fall guy.

Also, don't be that annoying guy or girl who asks all the questions. You know who I'm talking about—he or she may believe they impress everyone, but I guarantee you that they don't.

One out-of-state applicant unbelievably asked if he would get moving expenses covered if he was hired. I told him I'd give him a dollar for a bus ride to the local unemployment office if that's what he meant. Needless to say, he wasn't hired by my department. Though this particular applicant was not in a formal interview, as I explained earlier, everything is part of the interview process. My partner and I went to the local academy to present a badge to a recruit we decided to hire. We had the intention of making it special and prepared an informal presentation. At the conclusion of the badge ceremony, the recruit asked us if he was going to be reimbursed for already-paid academy expenses. My partner and I were blown away and began a rather memorable lecture regarding the benefits of a simple thank you followed by silence. I still remember the lack of common sense this new recruit had and how he ruined a positive moment by turning it into something negative. He no longer works for our department.

It seems that the recent trend in the academic world is to teach young people that they are supposed to ask questions during and at the end of the interview. Let me put it bluntly, nothing could be more wrong in public safety. I won't tell you how the civilian world feels about this practice, but in public safety, if you want a career, do not offend the interviewers by asking questions.

First, university professors are not considering the generation gap. Yes, twenty-year-olds are applying for the job, but forty-year-olds are interviewing them. Applicants will be evaluated by interviewers' standards. In addition, the interview will usually be conducted by a police sergeant or a fire captain who is not accustomed to answering questions from a subordinate. The interviewers should get to know the applicant, not the other way around, and the interview should not serve as a research tool. It's too late for that! Also, 90% of questions are comments in disguise or possess a specific agenda. Asking questions has on the possibility of a nominal upside, but a probability of committing a huge gaffe. It is not worth the risk, so don't do it.

Hopefully, you get my point. Do not ask questions at the conclusion of the interview—Ever.

Post-interview and Feedback

Drive to a safe location and write down everything that was asked and what you said in response. Continue thinking about your oral interview and how you can improve on any future oral examinations. If you fail the oral interview, some agencies offer feedback. Feedback is an overall evaluation of your interview. If you are courteous and respectful in making your request, the personnel representative may give you information and some golden nuggets on how you could improve. The reason for the agency offering feedback is to assist you in your improvement. If you've made it this far, chances are, you are a good candidate who just needs some polishing. It is not offered for you to gather information and use it against the city to file a lawsuit. If this were to ever happen, feedback would disappear for all applicants. It would also be counterproductive for you, as the agency that does eventually want you will turn and run during the background investigation.

If the organization does not offer feedback you will need to discover what you answered incorrectly by yourself. Ask officers and firefighters the questions you were asked and listen to their responses. The more you speak with the actual practitioners, the better understanding you will have of public safety. Ask them how they would have answered each question during an oral interview versus an actual situation and see if it's different. Ask them to give you additional scenarios and try to answer them without their assistance. Ask for a critique as most would be willing to help you and offer their infinite wisdom. However, do not take what each public safety official says as gospel. Evaluate what they tell you and develop your own mindset when handling situations.

Panel Review Clip

http://www.youtube.com/watch?v=2nTKdSMUrtM

Interviews
Practice. Practice. Practice.

The most important facet of doing well in the oral interview is to practice. Just as you practice anything else, you need to be willing to give 100% effort, which means wearing a business suit and answering oral questions. I suggest conducting what we call mock interviews several times prior to the actual interview. These mock interviews do not have to be with public safety officials. In fact, you can do them in your own living room with your wife or husband and/or friends and neighbors. I strongly suggest you make it as real as possible by going through all the motions you would go through in an actual oral interview. After you get done with your giggling it will be effective. Actually shake hands with your spouse or friend during the greeting and have a set of questions ready that they will ask you. You may even written the questions; it does not matter, the point is for you to get comfortable articulating yourself to another person and you get used to formulating a strategic way of thinking.

If you want to go all out (and you should), set up a video camera facing you from an interview's perspective. This will allow you to see what they see and hear what they hear. You will observe nuances you are unaware of, such as swaying side to side, turning your body and/or avoiding eye contact. You will hear all the "ums, ya knows, and yeahs" and other bothersome habits you may have.

You will see a major improvement between your first and last videotape and will be more likely to be successful in your interview. Applicants sometimes amaze me with their logic. They will spend two years in school when all they needed to do was spend two days on their oral interview preparation. Another way to improve, which is even more effective than videotaping, depending on your particular learning style, is a simple tape recorder. The more you speak into it and listen to yourself the more natural your oral interview will sound to the panel.

Conclusion

Never stop learning! Read and study every book in this series and you will be exponentially more prepared than you would be with any other method.

If you follow the advice of this book perhaps I will run into you while you are working as a fellow criminal justice professional. Participation in a criminal justice program is a noble endeavor and we thank you for your effort to make the world a better place.

Respectfully,
Sergeant Pete Bollinger